Take It As It Comes

The Life Story of Jennie de Boer Kuperus

CROOKED TREE
STORIES

Crooked Tree Stories Publishing Company

ISBN 978-1519741509

To my parents, Hendrik de Boer and Grietje Byzitter de Boer, who raised me and formed me

Christ is the Head of this House

The unseen Host at every meal
The silent Listener to every conversation

The Lord's My Shepherd
Psalter Hymnal #38

The Lord's my shepherd, I'll not want
He makes me down to lie
In pastures green He leadeth me
The quiet water by

My soul He doth restore again
And me to walk doth make
Within the paths of righteousness
E'en for His own Name's sake.

Yea, though I walk through death's dark vale
Yet will I fear no ill
For Thou art with me, and Thy rod
And staff me comfort still.

A table Thou hast furnished me
In presence of my foes
My head Thou dost with oil anoint
And my cup overflows.

Goodness and mercy all my life
Shall surely follow me
And in God's house forevermore
My dwelling place shall be.

Contents

Introduction

When I approached my mom about writing her life story, she claimed that she did not have much of a story to tell. While many of my perceptions about her were confirmed in writing this book, I learned much more than I expected.

Although I did not have the privilege of knowing my grandparents, I discovered that they, like my mom, had the ability to adapt to challenging circumstances. When Pake de Boer was faced with debt incurred during the Great Depression he defied oppressive laws in order to survive, and Beppe, my mom and her sisters displayed remarkable courage by assisting him. Pake served more than one term in a German-run labor camp during World War II.

Mom's early life was filled with challenges – a limited education, countless physically demanding jobs, losing her parents at a young age, immigrating to Canada alone in her early 20s, and learning a new language and way of life – yet she faced everything with resilience, determination, faith, and a complete lack of resentment. My parents and their siblings assimilated to life in America quickly. Although some left promising careers behind in the Netherlands, they considered any work that came their way opportunity enough.

Mom and Dad did not experience a romantic courtship, yet their marriage was a true partnership. When my mom recounts their farm experiences she does not romanticize or sugarcoat, but neither does she complain. They did the work that had to be done, side by side. There was little time for leisure or other pursuits, but they appreciated what they had without engaging in self-pity.

Mom has embraced the life she's been given. She selflessly raised five children and engages with her grandchildren on their level. She finds wonder in small things and has a quick, clever wit. There are too many comical stories involving Mom and Dad for this book, and it has been my intention to present my parents not only with humor, but also with due respect and sincerity. Neither has it been my intent to idealize our experiences. Farm life was a challenge, as was navigating the process of acculturation while simultaneously adhering to Dutch norms, and I was often ambivalent of my heritage. But listening to my mom's history has provided a broader understanding of what drove my parents, for which I am grateful.

One of Dad's favorite sayings was *ora et labora*, a Latin phrase meaning "pray and work." Our parents embodied that phrase, and the traits that carried them in adversity – their work ethic, devotion to God, pragmatism, frugality, faithfulness and service – also define them.

Although Mom and Dad did not have the benefit of higher education themselves, they understood its value, so my siblings and I were encouraged to attend college and travel wherever our jobs led us. When I asked my mom if she, too, had dreamed of an alternate career, she said in her characteristic nonchalant way that there had not been time for that – she lived day by day, and good work was always around the corner.

Many thanks to my family for piecing together details and making valuable contributions, especially Henriet Meyers for chronicling events with her camera; to Cynthia Kuperus for interviewing Mom in 2007, taping hours of conversation that became the baseline for this book; to Josh Epperly, Mike Kuperus, and Tracy Kuperus for editing; and to Tante Tiete for contributing details about the Kuperuses' World War II experiences. To my husband Mike, I appreciate your technical support but mostly your constant encouragement. Finally, I am grateful to my parents and their families for having the courage to uproot from their country and doing what it took to make it work. Their generation accomplished so much, yet they expected so little for themselves.

It turned out that Mom had quite a story to tell after all. This book was supposed to be a gift for her, but the gift has been mine.

Betty Kuperus Epperly
December 2015

"True humility is not thinking less of yourself; it is thinking of yourself less." - C.S. Lewis

The Netherlands, often referred to as Holland, is characterized by its unique landscape. Its name translates to "low countries;" half of its land lies below one meter above sea level. An extensive system of dykes and dams is in place to prevent flooding. Since the 16th century, large areas of land have been reclaimed from the sea and lakes through peat extraction. Each of the twelve Dutch provinces has its own government, unique customs and history.

Most of the province of Friesland is located on the mainland, but it also includes the West Friesland Islands. Frisian natives speak their own language, known as West Frisian. The seven red water lilies (or pompeblêden, as they are called in Frisian) on the Frisian flag are a reference to the Frisian "sea countries" in the Middle Ages: independent regions that were allied against the Vikings.

Early Life in Friesland

My father, Hendrik de Boer, was born on December 21, 1898, in the town of Garyp, located in the Dutch province of Friesland. He was the firstborn son of Folkert and Tryntje de Boer; then came Linze, Pieter, Johannes, Dirk, Frederik and Jaike, the only girl. My grandfather, or *Pake*, as we called him, was a successful farmer, and the family often moved when better opportunities came. My grandmother (*Beppe*) de Boer had diabetes and was often in poor health. The name de Boer was fitting; it means "farmer."

Folkert and Tryntje de Boer, circa 1950

My mother's surname was Byzitter, which means "sit by you." My mom, Grietje Byzitter, was born on January 27, 1900, to Sipke and Grietje Byzitter in the town of Boerakker, located in the province of Groningen. She had one older brother, Hendrik. Her other siblings were Jan, Jantje, Teitje, Geeske, Jacob, Fokkeline, and Berendina. I remember Beppe Byzitter to be such a sweet lady. Pake Byzitter worked very hard on his farm in Haulerwyk.

My mom's school photo, circa 1910. She is slightly to the left of and slightly higher than center, wearing a dark dress with a white yoke, one of the only children who is smiling.

Napoleon Bonaparte of France abolished the Kingdom of Holland and annexed it in 1810. Holland had previously been ruled by Napoleon's brother, King Louis (Lodewijk) Bonaparte, who established a monetary system using the guilder.

Previously, surnames were not required, but Napoleon decreed that all births, deaths and marriages be registered with surnames. The Dutch initially used a patronymic system in which the father's first name became the first son's last name, and other children were named after other ancestors. In the 1600s people began to turn the patronymic name into modern last names: Jan Hendricksen (Jan the son of Hendrick) gave his son the surname Hendricksen instead of Jansen. A suffix was often added to indicate 'son of' or 'daughter of.' For example, Jan, son of Hendrick would be written Jan Hendricks, Jan Hendrickse or Jan Hendricksen. Many patronymics did become permanent family names, such as today's very common Peters, Hansen, etc. Other family names were related to personal qualities or appearance. The prefixes "de" and "van" are used to indicate occupations or regions of origin.

Consistent with the Dutch independent mind, pragmatism, stubbornness, and sense of humor, thousands of Dutch did not take Napoleon seriously. Perhaps they wanted to rebel or mock him. Additionally, they looked at this name system as a temporary law to be repealed once Napoleon left Holland, so they deliberately adopted and registered family names that sound ridiculous. Some examples: Suikerbuik (Sugar belly); Spring in 't Veld (Jump in the Field); Uiekruier (Onion-crier); Naaktgeboren (Born naked); Schooier (Beggar, tramp); Scheefnek (Crooked-neck); and Rotmensen (Rotten people). However, Napoleon's civil registration system stuck, and so did the names.

My father enlisted in the Dutch army at the age of 18. While home on leave, the maid met Dad at the door and told him he had a new baby brother. When he later told us this story he would say that he "almost went through the ground" with shock. This baby only survived a few months, so

Hendrik Byzitter and Hendrik de Boer

Dad came home on furlough for the funeral. He served in the army with my mother's brother, Hendrik, in Assen, Drenthe. Hendrik Byzitter invited Dad to the Byzitter home for a meal. My father took an interest in my mother and wrote this letter, now in my possession: "Dear Grietje: I have in mind that I would like to visit you. If I do not hear back from you I will come to your house this Sunday night." My mother was fine with this so she did not reply.

My parents' engagement picture

My parents dated for two years and were married on May 3, 1923. First they had to go to the public court to make it official, but the actual wedding ceremony took place the following Sunday in church. Like their parents, my mother and father were dairy farmers. They first lived in a nice little house in the woods in Haule, Friesland.

The Dutch custom was to name the first son after the father's parents and the first daughter after the mother's parents. Subsequent children were named after other relatives. My oldest sister, named Grietje after my mom's mother, was born in 1925. Tryntje, named after my paternal grandmother, followed in 1929.

At this time my father's brother, Pieter, wanted to share a farm with Dad because he did not get along with Pake de Boer. Dad agreed, so the family moved to a new farm a couple of miles away. This farm was much bigger, but as my dad would find out later, the land was not good for growing things.

My parents' first home

I was born on March 9, 1931, and was named Jantje after my mother's oldest sister. I was born at home, as most babies were in those days. My sister Grietje had stayed with my grandparents during my home delivery, and when she returned my mom said, "Grietje, this is your new sister."

Grietje held up her new doll and said, "Yes, but look what I have. When I put money in my dolly she sticks her tongue out!" She liked her new dolly more than her new sister. Since there were six years between Grietje and me, I always played with Tryntje, who was closer to my age.

Uncle Pieter got married in the mid-1930s and bought his own place. By this time the Great Depression was in full swing in our country, and my parents had a very hard time moneywise, taking on a lot of debt that they had to work off later.

The home in which I was born in Haulerwyk, Friesland

In the United States, the Stock Market Crash on September 20, 1929, marks the beginning of the Great Depression, but in the Netherlands the depression gained momentum more gradually. The years between 1933 and 1936 were a period of severe economic crisis. The depression lasted longer in the Netherlands than in most countries, partly because of the refusal to drop the gold standard. Economic hardships resulted in riots and political instability, and can be linked to the rise of the Dutch fascists, the Nationaal-Sociaistische Beweging (NSB).

On his own, Dad could not support our family on the big farm. One day, while doing business at the farmers market, he met a man from Surhuisterveen, Friesland, who had just lost his wife. The man and his grown son were looking for a housekeeper, and it seemed like a good opportunity, so we moved in with them. My mother did the housekeeping and cooking, and in return we could use some of his land and keep our cows in the barn.

The house was full of fleas; Mom had to go on her knees and scrub the floors like mad, even in the attic. She put something in the water that was supposed to kill the fleas – I don't know what it was, but it was smelling like crazy.

We were used to biking and walking everywhere, but this man had a car. To start it, you had to crank a handle. Sometimes he would give us rides, which was a big treat.

My sisters and I shared a bed, and I was in the middle. In order to fit, we all had to sleep on our sides, knees under bottoms. Tryntje was a thumb sucker for a long time. In the middle of the night I would reach my hand around to her mouth, and she started right away sucking my thumb.

Me and Tryntje, 1937, at our grandparents' farm in Haulerwyk

We had no electricity or running water in our homes so we used lanterns, even in the barn. Rainwater that dripped from our roof was caught in a cistern for later use. We had a little cup on the kitchen shelf that everyone used for drinking. One time when I was thirsty I saw that it contained clear liquid, and it looked good to me so I drank it. It turned out to be bleach.

People in the country had a sponge bath once a week. My aunt had problems with her hair falling out. She washed it every nine months, so maybe that is why. We must not have smelled like roses, but we didn't know any better since everyone was the same.

On some farms a water pump outside the barn made it easier to give cows a drink. In the winter when they stayed in the barn we filled buckets at the well for them.

There were many canals in the Netherlands, and since the land was very low, windmills were used to pump out water. They were also used to make paper as well as wooden planks. My uncle and aunt were the caretakers of a windmill in Friesland. Once, while climbing to the top, my aunt had a terrible scare when she almost lost her balance.

Instead of going to stores for food, the baker came every other day to our door by bike. We could buy a whole loaf of bread, or a half or a quarter. A grocer came door to door also. We told him what we needed and he got the groceries from a basket on his bike. When we paid him, sometimes he would give us a handful of candies.

Many women canned vegetables, but my mom did not. Ice boxes were not common in the Dutch countryside, so we stored fruits and vegetables in our *kelder*, or basement. A stairway in the hall led to this storage area, which was lined with shelves. Large barrels filled with salt brine preserved our beans and other vegetables.

Breakfast was a simple meal of *brij* (oatmeal), and maybe some dark rye bread. The bread was buttered and put in front of us on the table. We used plates only when necessary, because in order to wash dishes we had to heat water from the cistern. Sometimes we put Edam or Gouda cheese on the bread, but this was considered a delicacy.

Our big meal was at the noon hour – meat and vegetables, and always potatoes since we grew them in our fields. We boiled them and added gravy and salt. Sometimes we had *op bakte iepeltjes* – we sliced the boiled potatoes and fried them in a pan until they were nice and crispy. Other days we made *stamppot* – boiled potatoes mixed with kale or carrots and sausage or bacon. We made our version of pancakes *(pannekoeken)* by frying a batter of flour, eggs, salt and milk. *Snert* was a thick pea soup mixed with sausage, bacon or ham. Dessert was *soep'n brij*, which was porridge made of buttermilk and barley. The most deluxe dessert was *pareltje brij*, a mixture of barley, buttermilk, raisins and some kind of sweet red sauce, served cold.

Our evening meal was simple, often more potatoes and whatever else was on hand. In the summertime we ate fruit that we grew, such as grapes and apples.

On Sundays we sometimes had an egg for breakfast. A special dessert after our noon meal was either vanilla pudding or a

cookie. We couldn't bake since we had no ovens, so the cookies must have come from the baker. We never went to a restaurant, but we always had plenty to eat.

A dry goods store, Surhuisterveen, 1940

We cooked on a *klomkachel,* which was a high, narrow stove in the middle of the kitchen. In winter when we woke up in the morning we lit the fire and kept it going all day long, filling the stove with wood, coal or turf. In the summer we cooked in a shed next to the barn that had a table and chairs, as well as a stove.

We were not instructed about dental hygiene. Some families shared a communal toothbrush, attached by a chain to the water pump outside. We only saw the dentist if we had a big problem. If a tooth was painful, it was pulled out with no anesthesia.

A doctor visit was rare. If we got sick, we just had to wait to get better. Because I had sore throats all the time my mom took me to a doctor, who said I needed my tonsils taken out. We went by bike to a clinic in Drachten – Mom pedaled and I sat on a metal seat that was over the back wheel. While I waited for my turn I heard horrible noises next door where the surgery was being performed on someone else. Patients were given some anesthesia, but that didn't stop the complaining. After the surgery we waited a few hours until most of the bleeding had stopped, and then we went back home on the bike. In my case, the doctor did not remove everything, so after I immigrated to Canada another doctor finished the job.

*Me and Tryntje, Boelenslaan
Christian School, 1940*

The school year in the Netherlands began on April 1. We did not have preschool or kindergarten in the country like they did in the city, so our education began when we were six years old. In August we had three weeks vacation, and we looked forward the whole year for that. My sisters had gone to school for about eight months in Haulerwyk. We had moved to Surhuisterveen in December when the weather was bad. Since the school was quite far away and Tryntje had to recuperate from having bad headaches, my parents kept my sisters home until April.

We went to the Boelenslaan Christian School, which was free to all church members. Since Tryntje had gone only a partial year in Haulerwyk she had to start over, so she and I were both in first grade. She outdid me in everything, maybe because of her head start or because she was older. She had nice handwriting; I was the opposite. Although she was smarter in every subject, she was not proud of it and was always kind to me.

Our school was divided into three rooms. We sat on benches, two to a desk. Inkpots were built into the desks, but young students wrote with pencils. We could not speak to kids seated next to us, even if we needed help. For morning prayers and Bible lessons we folded our hands and listened attentively. Every day we sang folk songs and hymns, standing up with hands folded behind our backs. If we had a question or had to go to the outhouse we raised a finger and waited to be called on.

Since it was assumed that girls would become housewives, we were taught mending, embroidery and knitting twice a week for an hour while the boys did arithmetic. I didn't like working with thread and yarn because I couldn't get it going. One day the class was especially no good and the teacher said, "Hey, if you want to be like that you can go to the boys." I loved arithmetic so I said, "Oh, I would love that!" and boy, did I get a slap on my face – my whole cheek was red. Trietje cried because I was mistreated, but in those days that's what you got and you didn't say anything about it.

My seatmate was a neighbor boy, Johann de Vries, who was also good at math. After we worked through a complicated problem with many steps we saw that we had different answers. I said, "Let me see yours," and I checked his work. It looked perfect, so I changed my answer. But he had copied the problem wrong from the board, and when the teacher checked our work she could tell I was the guilty one. From then on we did not consult one another.

On August 31, Queen Wilhelmina's birthday, we had special activities and games in school. We walked arm in arm around the school, singing, and had wagon rides. Everyone wore something orange – girls might wear an orange hair ribbon and boys would wear orange ties or armbands – because the royal family's last name was Oranje.

Wilhelmina (Wilhelmina Helena Pauline Maria: August 31, 1880 – November 28, 1962) was Queen of the Netherlands from 1890 to 1948. Her reign of nearly 58 years was longer than any other Dutch monarch. She served during both world wars, the economic crisis of 1933, and the decline of the Netherlands as a major colonial power. Respected by her constituents and world leaders alike, she is primarily remembered for her role in World War II, in which she proved to be a great inspiration to the Dutch resistance.

During recess when the weather was nice we played different kinds of tag, but marbles was the favorite activity. For a penny you could buy 20 *knikkers*, or clay marbles. When they were new they were beautiful shades of blue and green. We would try to shoot the marble into someone's pot, and if we missed, the other person could keep the marble. At home in the winter we played games with Mom. We drew lines on our wooden calendar base to form nine squares and used buttons to play tic-tac-toe.

Since we lived about 30 kilometers away from our relatives we did not see them very often. In the summer we would go to our cousins' houses, and then they would stay with us. Sometimes we walked to a *deerentuin,* a park with animals, a playground and an ice cream stand. Having ice cream just once a year made it very special.

My cousins and me. I am in the back row with a bow.
Picture taking was serious business, but I must have
thought something was funny.

We also stayed with Pake and Beppe de Boer in the summer. They were devout Christians, and prayer and Bible reading were a part of each meal. In those days only ministers and church elders prayed aloud. Pake was very stern, and his silent prayers seemed ever so long to us kids. We all folded our hands and prayed to ourselves, but we had to wait for Pake to finish before we could begin eating. We would open one eye to sneak a peak every so often.

He had a habit of yawning during prayer time, and usually after the third yawn his prayer was finished. One time when I was about five years old, I refused the food at the table and was sent to a stall in the barn as punishment. I wanted nothing to do with this so I took off, but Pake and Beppe found me before I went too far.

In 1938 the man we were staying with got married so our housekeeping services were no longer needed. My dad bought a little farm in Ureterp, also in Friesland. The barn had a room in the front that was our living area, which was quite common in the Netherlands. It was very convenient – you opened the door at the back of the room, and there were the cows. Also in the main living area were two bed stays – beds on hinges that had to be pulled down from a hole in the wall – one for my parents and one for the girls.

There is a Dutch saying that someone is from the "*hak op de tak,*" or the heel of the tree, when he is always quickly going from one place to the next. That was my dad. He was always eager to try something new, unlike his brothers, who liked to stick with what they knew and play it safe. Our family was unique in many ways because of Dad's methods, and my mom was easygoing, supporting him in everything. They were good partners.

All of us had lots of chores. My mother always helped with the milking and in every step of fieldwork, never complaining. Tryntje was goodness herself. She liked the house clean and would do it without being asked. Since my dad had no sons, my sisters and I helped on the farm also.

In the spring when the cows were put outside we cleaned the stalls and stanchions. We scrubbed and scrubbed the bricks and put white sand between them. Each stall held two cows, with boards in between. When Tryntje and I were too young to help in the fields we made a playhouse out of one of the stalls, pretending that one side was the dining room and the other side was a kitchen. We often played with dolls, and we wanted to feed them, so we opened their mouths and forced a little buttermilk inside. They started to stink, but we still played with them and had a good time.

As we grew older our responsibilities increased. We had about ten acres of good soil on our farm. In the spring we planted potatoes. With a special tool, Dad would dig a hole in the ground that was just the right size. We followed behind with the potatoes, which we carried in bags around our necks. After we put one in each hole we tamped down the dirt with our wooden shoe. When the potatoes were in the fields we were extra careful when we let the cows out, leading them around the crops. The potatoes would multiply over the summer, and during fall harvest time Dad loosened the ground with a fork. Our job was to be on our knees and pull the potatoes out of the mud. We put them in baskets that Dad would later transfer to the wagon.

We also grew wheat. During harvest time Dad cut the stalks with a scythe, and we rolled them into sheaths. Hay was also cut by hand. All of us would line up in a row, except for Grietje, who was already working as a housekeeper for another family. Tryntje was not so strong, so she was first in line. She rolled the cut hay, and when it came to me I rolled it a little more; then my mother rolled it to my father. These bunches were put in little rows, and every day we loaded some on the horse-drawn wagon for the cows. The ground was very uneven, and if the wagon tipped we had to start over. Later on we made heaps of hay with pitchforks, and when Grietje was home she could stack it up so high. One time she drank dirty water and got typhus, which was highly contagious. While she recuperated I took over her job, but I was not nearly as strong.

Our eight cows had to be milked twice a day. The stronger family members milked the cows that were harder to milk, and I got the easy milkers. Grietje milked cows before she went to school, even before she was a teenager. In nice weather we milked the cows outside after leading them to a special corner. We sat on a stool with a pail between our knees and tied a rope around one of the cows' hind legs to keep it from kicking the pail. Their tails were tied along with the leg because they used them to slap the flies, and sometimes we would also be on the receiving end. Nowadays farmers have machines that keep the milk cool, but since we had no electricity we boiled our milk before we drank it.

We kept pigs in a little shed, and banty hens walked freely on our land. We did not eat the hens, but sometimes we found their hiding spots where they laid their eggs. Lots of cats roamed around too, catching mice for us. Since Mom was a cat lover, we could let them inside the house. Grietje would twirl her hair with one hand and stroke a cat with the other. She also trained a dog to pull a cart and put me in the cart for rides when I was quite small. The dog got loose and ran off once, but the cart kept going down the hill with me in it. Some people rescued me before I crashed.

There was no road in front of our home, just a bike path and a waterway beyond. Although ships used this waterway, motors were not allowed. Poles were used to steer and push the ships through, and the ladies would be like horses, wearing a harness and pulling as hard as they could. My grandmother had this job when she was a teenager. Once when a ship delivered something to us I played the role of the "horse" – I pulled the ship while a man on the stern steered with a pole.

The cows' milk was put in a metal can and left by the waterway, where a boat from the milk factory picked it up. Milk cans were returned later with money in an envelope tucked in the lid. We never heard of anybody stealing money in those days. If we wanted buttermilk or whey (for the pigs and cows) we ordered it from the factory and the boat would drop it off on the bank.

I learned to swim in the waterway. One time a neighbor man stood on the other side and said, "Come to me, you can do it!" I struggled quite a bit and got caught in the current, but I made it.

School was about a mile away, and in the wintertime when the water froze we could skate to school. Our skates were not like the ones you see today. We strapped these wooden blades to our socks, so when we got to school our feet were cold. Our wet socks were laid to dry on the furnace. Everyone had an assigned cubbyhole for their wooden shoes, which were not to be worn indoors because they were so noisy.

During the rest of the school year we walked to school with our neighbors. We had to cross a bridge, where a group of boys from the public school would sometimes wait for us. There was always a little war – they called us *fijn duivels* (fine devils), and we called them *barbarian duivels*. The boys fought each other, and though the girls were not involved, I was terrified. Sometimes kids threw wooden shoes at each other, but then the other side would take them. So in those days, it was dangerous just to get to school.

Before the Middle Ages, shoes were worn only by elitists in the Netherlands. Since wooden shoes could be made out of a single piece of wood, they became a solid, practical and inexpensive way to protect one's feet in the moist Dutch climate.

In the early 1900s wooden shoes were smoothed and finished with carvings and decorations, which differed from region to region. Shoe shapes were different for men and women. Men's wooden shoes typically were black or yellow, and women's shoes often featured elaborate painted designs. When industrial shoe manufacturing increased, demand for wooden shoes decreased, but they were still the most common choice in the countryside for some time. During World Wars I and II there was a resurgence in the popularity of wooden shoes because leather was in short supply. Even after World War II, a shoemaker could be found in most villages. Wooden shoes may occasionally still be seen on the countryside, worn by gardeners, farmers, or tradesmen.

We each had one outfit for school. Many of our clothes were knitted, I suppose because yarn was cheaper than fabric. My grandmother was an excellent knitter, and she made beautiful sweaters and skirts for us. My sisters and I never wore pants, even when we rode bikes.

On Sundays we wore regular shoes to church and a special dress. After the morning milking we went to the early church service on our bikes. In the winter the klomkachel had to be loaded all the time, otherwise the house would be cold, so mothers with small kids did not always go to church. After lunch we went to the second service. Sundays were a day of rest.

Me and my friend, Renskje

When we were older we attended weekly catechism classes after school. Our minister was blind in his left eye, so the boys who were not prepared to recite their memory work would rush to sit on his left side. In this position they could look at their book when it was their turn without the minister noticing.

On December 6 we celebrated *Sinterklaas Day,* or St. Nicholas Day. It was said that St. Nicholas came to each house on December 5 at night on a white horse, and we sure believed in him. We put hay in our wooden shoes and left them on the stoop in case the horse was hungry. Sometimes an adult rode a horse around the village at night so that kids would see hoof prints the next morning.

In the morning we would search for the present that Mom and Dad hid for us. One year Tryntje and I each got a doll. My mom and Grietje had knitted clothes for our dolls as an extra surprise, but I was not happy to see that Tryntje's doll wore a dress while mine wore boys' clothes.

Later in the day as we sat in the kitchen area we would see a hand come around the corner (probably my dad's) and throw *pepernoten* (gingersnaps) on the floor. Gingerbread men were also part of the celebration. One year during the war Dad came in the house and pretended to be upset because there was no gingerbread left for him. He said, "Next time I will not leave the house until I get some!" Just then, my mom came around the corner with a gingerbread man as wide as the table. Since we grew our own wheat we could bring flour to the bakery for extra goodies, and my parents had ordered this custom treat to surprise us.

On December 6 in the Netherlands, Sinterklaas, dressed in his red bishop robes, parades through the streets on his white horse accompanied by his helper, Zwarte Piet (Black Peter). Legend has it that Zwarte Piet's face is black because he is a Moor from Spain. Some say that his face is blackened with soot because he has to climb through chimneys to deliver gifts for Sinterklaas. In recent years, Zwarte Piet has become a controversial figure – some claim he is a simply an innocent part of their cultural heritage, while others see the character as an insult to their ancestry.

Before going to bed on December 5, children put their wooden shoes next to the chimney of the coal-fired stove. They may put a carrot or some hay in the shoe and a bowl of water nearby for Sinterklaas' horse. The next day they find some candy or a small present in their shoes. Poems from Sinterklaas usually accompany gifts, bearing a personal message for the receiver. It is usually a humorous poem, which often teases the recipient for well-known bad habits or other character deficiencies.

On December 25, which we called the first day of Christmas, we celebrated Jesus' birth with a church service. On the second day of Christmas (December 26) we went to another service. The *Gereformeerde Kerk*, or Christian Reformed Church, to which we belonged, could not have Christmas trees (I suppose because they were seen as an idol), but they were allowed in the *Herformeert*, the Reformed Church.

Gereformeerde Kerk, Surhuisterveen, circa 1940

Once we went to a Christmas party at the Reformed Church and saw real candles burning in the tree. A man had to stand next to it and put the candles on one by one, making sure the tree did not burn. Some people in our town had a little tree in their house. We put some greenery above our mirror and placed cotton on top for the "snow."

On December 31 it was the custom to make *oliebollen*. We mixed flour, eggs, raisins and other ingredients and dropped spoonsful of the batter into hot oil. They tasted like doughnuts when we rolled them in sugar. My mom could not stand the smell, so we girls took over. Lots of visitors came to our home to celebrate the new year. My parents were both great storytellers, so lots of laughter filled our house.

World War II: Challenging Years

In 1940 the Netherlands became involved in World War II. Dutch soldiers fought against the Germans for five days because we did not want to join them, but Germany had a strong army and soon German troops were stationed in our town. Little kids did not know what it meant, and it was stressful for everyone. I was nine years old, too young to understand.

With the advent of World War I in September of 1939 the Netherlands maintained a policy of neutrality. While many of their neighbors fell to the Germans, the Netherlands remained outside the war. The country's hope for neutrality was bolstered by a promise of nonaggression made by Hitler. However, this assurance proved worthless. On May 10, 1940, the German army began its invasion of the Netherlands. Despite valiant efforts made on the part of the Dutch military, the Netherlands fell to the

Rotterdam, post-invasion

29

Germans after only five days of fighting. After the bombing of Rotterdam, the Dutch capitulated. Persecuted Jews who had initially fled to the Netherlands as a safe harbor were shocked. For those five days, many attempted to flee the country.

At the time of Holland's capitulation, about 140,000 Jews resided in the Netherlands. By the time of the war's end, the Nazis had deported 107,000 Jews out of Holland. Of these, only 5000 survived to return home following the war and 30,000 managed to survive in hiding or by other means.

The Germans took all the radios they could find because they did not want people to know what was going on in the war. Our family never had a radio; those who owned one had to put it in a special hiding place.

We heard that people were picked up on the streets, which was scary. Dutch young men who were 18 and older were forced to serve in the German army or work in their ammunition factories. Young men whose families owned farms did not have to go to Germany because the food that was produced on the farms was needed for German soldiers. These young farmers were issued a special document called an *Ausweis* to prove to soldiers that they were exempt.

Many of our relatives were farmers, so most of our male cousins did not have to go to Germany. Since our family had three girls, we were not forced to help the Germans. My dad had sometimes joked that Grietje, being so strong on the farm, was his "boy," but now he said he was so glad she was a girl.

One of Pake de Boer's farm hands had to serve in the German army, so Grietje went to live with Pake and Beppe for several years. Every day Grietje and Pake peeled lots of potatoes since they were now eaten for breakfast, lunch and dinner. Pake did not talk much unless he was relaxed and most people were afraid of him, but during these times together he told Grietje lots of stories about his childhood. He told her that when he was dating Beppe he had to walk ever so many miles to see her since he had no bike. Later, when he finally had a bike, someone offered him a ride in a

Pake and Beppe de Boer's house

car but he refused because he thought they were so dangerous. Besides helping in the house, Grietje helped my grandfather milk the cows. By this time, Beppe's diabetes had progressed. Grietje gave her insulin shots, but she became weaker and died of a heart attack.

Dutch men who were forced to help the Germans did not go willingly, and many found hiding places in other homes to avoid service. Although it was dangerous to hide these men, called *onderduikers*, my parents felt it was our duty to help those in need. For a time we hid two boys at our home. They slept in a box on a wagon that we kept in the ditch at the back of our field.

Much of our good food went to the Germans. Dutch citizens were given ration coupons; my mom would go once a month to pick up the new batch. Even though we had ration coupons for the bakery, bakers could not get the ingredients (like sugar and yeast) they needed to make the food taste good. Bread was hard as a rock and black as tar.

My mom loved coffee and always had a pot on the stove. When this, too, was rationed she used the grounds over and over again. She tried to make coffee out of crushed chestnuts. This really did not taste like coffee at all, but it was hot liquid, and we just had to use our imaginations.

Those who hid onderduikers shared their rationed food with them. One of the young men at our house could eat like a horse, but we had lots of potatoes and plenty of milk, so we were better off than most. In the wartime, all the good land had to be used for growing potatoes because of food shortages. My dad earned $750 by growing potatoes for other people. This was good money, but our land was damaged because we could no longer rotate crops. Since we could no longer grow grass we could not feed the cows, so we had goats instead. We could drink their milk and they ate hardly anything.

Onderduikers, Groningen, 1943

People in the provinces of Friesland, Groningen and Drenthe had more food because these were areas rich in farmland. People from cities would sometimes come to our doors with money, looking for food, but even that was risky for them. If they were stopped on the return trip on their bikes, the food could be taken away. A girl from Amsterdam stayed with us for a while because her family was starving. We also boarded a boy who was 16 and could not find a job. We couldn't pay him wages, but we could feed him. Because food was so scarce, the black market came into being.

The black market was a response to food rationing during World War II. As German U-boats patrolled the Atlantic Ocean, food imports to the Netherlands became restricted. The government imposed rations in an effort to give all citizens a fair share of what was available. The black market emerged due to the inevitable market gap. Farmers and butchers supplied much of the black market food. Although some price gouging was inevitable, others who participated worked in conjunction with the Dutch Resistance. Customers had no incentive to inform authorities since the items that were supplied were often necessary for survival. Those who were caught faced stiff penalties as well as prison sentences. Prisoners who were sent to German-run work camps were often severely mistreated.

At the market my father met a man named Dirk Boonestroo who was from Nunspeet, Gelderland. I don't know why, but Mr. Boonestroo needed a place to hide, so Dad invited him to stay with us. We were shocked because Dirk would say, "Oh my God" all the time, and if you are not used to hearing that phrase you are more sensitive to it. We knew that he belonged to the Christian Reformed Church. My mother asked, "Jantje, do you think he is a Christian?" and I said, "No, because he always takes God's name in vain." After three months at our place he was "cured."

One day Dirk received a letter and shouted, "They shot the *opper* dead!" This meant that the traitor (NSBer) who lived in his town and knew of his secret activities was shot, so he could go home. He was so happy to be able to join his family.

The Germans came around to look for onderduikers and sometimes had help from NSBers. The NSB was a political party that was formed in the beginning of the war. They thought it would be wonderful if the Netherlands were part of Germany. We did not know who belonged to the NSB, so we couldn't trust anybody. They got money from the Nazis for squeaking on those who were hiding. Then there would be a *razzia* (raid) at the home, and the Germans would take the onderduikers into custody. In our neighborhood watch program, people would volunteer a couple of hours each night, and if they saw Germans they would warn the rest of us.

The NSB was the only legal political party in the Netherlands for much of the war. NSBers sympathized and collaborated with Germany. Every new mayor appointed during German occupation belonged to the NSB, and in 1941, when German victory seemed imminent, about 3% of Dutch males had also joined. The NSB was outlawed after the Germans surrendered on May 6, 1945.

Farmers had to register their animals and were sometimes ordered by the Germans to kill a pig or a cow. They could keep some meat for themselves and share some with neighbors, but most had to be shipped for German soldiers. One of my uncles hid an unregistered pig in a crate under the hay, and one day it escaped. My cousin yelled, "Dad, the 'silent' pig is on the loose!" It was soon recaptured. As long as you had good neighbors who understood what you were doing, you came to no harm for failing to register animals.

My father still had much debt from the depression, and he did not register many of his animals. Sometimes he would kill a pig in our barn and give some meat to hungry people; he also sold meat on the black market in Drachten for $1.00 a pound. This was more than people paid at the butcher shop before the war, but during the war the prices went up for everything. One of our neighbors said to Dad, "I know what you are doing!" so from then on we hid the unregistered pigs in the back of the field.

Sometimes I would make deliveries of this black market meat on my bike to Drachten. People would pay with money or a piece of clothing. On one trip, riding my bike on a narrow pathway next to the waterway, I slipped and fell in the water, meat and all. I was okay, but the meat became a very expensive lunch for the fish.

Through Dirk Boonestroo my dad made connections to sell "black horses," (unregistered stock) in Overijessel. Just as Germans took other livestock from farmers for their own use, they also took horses. Farmers who received a notice that their horse was to be surrendered were heartbroken because they were very close to their beloved animals. Many would go to great lengths to keep them. They would come to my dad and describe their horse's color and markings. Dad would buy a horse on the black market that looked similar, and then in the dark of night he would bring it to the farmer. This "imposter" horse would be delivered to the Germans.

My sister Grietje helped Dad deliver the horses, sometimes by herself. When she traveled overnight she would ask people if she could stay in their shed. Once when she was taking a horse to Overijssel she was stopped by the authorities. Since the horse had no papers, the officers snagged it. Grietje had to walk home carrying the saddle, and my father was fined.

Eventually, after several infractions regarding his black market activities my father was sentenced to a work camp in Ommen, Overijssel, for three months. He was one of the lucky ones. Other people at the camp, such as Jews and political prisoners, were tortured. My father and others who were convicted of black market activities and other economic crimes were not treated so poorly.

The German commander asked my father if he knew how to harvest potatoes, but at first Dad did not understand him. When the question was translated, Dad said he had lots of experience. He and other farmers were picked up every morning, brought to potato farms to work all day, and returned to the camp at night. Germans considered farmers a valuable resource. It was fortunate that Dad served his sentence in the fall during the harvest season. If he had served in the winter, he would not have had this opportunity.

Harvesting potatoes was hard work, but my dad was used to that. One time another worker said to him, "Hey, boer, you forgot a row!" This man could not keep up with his rows so he tried to make my dad do his work and was later punished for his trickery. My dad and other field workers were fed very well by the Dutch landowners. When they returned to the camp and received their food rations, Dad gave his portion to the Jews and other hungry prisoners because his belly was full.

Another advantage was that we could now have contact with my father. The farmers told us that Dad was working for them, and Grietje rode on a horse to bring him food and letters from home. My mom once wrote, "The cats keep having babies," which was a code so that Dad would know his black market stock were reproducing.

When Dad was released after serving his three-month sentence he told us how he had witnessed the torture of ministers who were at the same camp and had felt helpless because he could not intervene. Although he was relieved to be home, he continued with his black market activities. He served two more shorter sentences during the war.

Arbeitseinsatzslager Erika (Work Procurement Camp Erica) was a prison camp located near the village of Ommen, Overijssel, close to the German border. Before the war, the camp had been used by followers of a religious cult, but when all religious movements were dissolved by the Nazis the camp became German property. When Werner Schwier was appointed on June 13, 1941, to the position of camp Commandant of Ommen, his first task was to hire 48 camp guards, called Kontroll Kommando, or KK.

Most prisoners at the camp were black marketeers and butchers who were found guilty of the Food Rationing Act of 1939. Other prisoners had shown resistance to occupational authorities. Only eight prisoners were Jewish. After the initiation process, the prisoners were assigned to work details. They slept in hammocks, three high. Bedding, clothing and food were insufficient. The prisoners were forced to do hard labor with a constant threat of being beaten. The KK became notorious for their brutality, leading Dutch judges to eventually refuse to send convicts to the camp.

Prisoner and KK guard

Two of the Jewish prisoners were killed. One survivor wrote, "Erika was the most horrible camp I stayed during the war. In no other camp I was so systematically physically abused, every day, as in Ommen."

Werner Schwier was arrested after the war but escaped from a Belgium internment camp. He fled to Germany, where he died in 1971. He was never prosecuted.

After my father returned home, my uncle came to ask him a favor. His relatives, a family with three daughters, were being evacuated from their home in Gelderland, and they needed to be picked up and transported to the Kuperus farm in Friesland. To complicate matters further, the mother had tuberculosis. My uncle offered to lend my father his fancy horse and buggy for the trip.

Because food was more available in rural areas of the Netherlands during World War II, those in farming communities were less susceptible to contagious diseases. Living quarters in the city were cramped because so many homes had been destroyed and many families shared residences. Besides facing food shortages, urban Dutch families had a lack of clean water. Linens and dishes could not be not washed properly; waste disposal was ineffective, and bathing was infrequent. Amsterdam experienced a 208% increase in tuberculosis diagnosis between 1939 and 1945. Another disease was typhoid fever, which is highly contagious and prevalent in individuals who eat contaminated food. By 1942 the Netherlands was experiencing five times more cases of typhoid fever than before.

My father took out the map and saw that Gelderland was very far away, but he agreed to my uncle's request and planned to deliver some black horses on the same trip. Dad told Grietje she could not come along due to the risk involved, but fearless as ever, she insisted. It took a long time to get there, and it was dangerous because of all of the bombing in the cities. Even the horses were spooked by the incredible noise. Dad and Grietje delivered the horses and picked up the family the next day.

The TB-infected mother was in a tent next to her family's house, and on the door of the house was a sign that read, "TB patient," so Germans stayed away. The family boarded the buggy, and on the trip back to Friesland my dad picked up a hitchhiker. The police stopped the buggy, searched everyone, and found a gun on the hitchhiker. My father was very angry that the man had put them in danger. The hitchhiker was arrested, but my dad and the others were allowed to continue. When they arrived at the Kuperus home, the poor horse collapsed because of the long journey and did not get up for six days. A makeshift gazebo had been set up by health authorities next to the house so the mother could be quarantined.

Many people from the city had to be evacuated when bombs destroyed their homes. Displaced people were often housed by Frisian families. My aunt and uncle had six kids of their own but they took in three evacuees. I remember my aunt as someone who was always laughing, even in these circumstances. She sometimes traded milk and butter for yarn and fabric, which she kept in a closet in the back of the barn. One day she went to visit a sick friend. When she returned the evacuees were told they could go home, so she and uncle brought them back. The next time my aunt opened her secret closet she saw that all of her goodies were gone. The evacuees had stolen everything.

Every night planes came from England and cut over our area to bomb Germany. We heard them in the sky and couldn't sleep. It was always the same noise, night after night, but we never got used to it.

We had curfews at night; the Germans did not want the planes to know if they were flying over the country or the city, so we were told to put black paper on our windows so that no light would shine through. One winter night a British plane dropped a bomb by accident on the other side of the waterway in an old lady's yard. The ground shook with the horrible noise. Two miles away from our house, some British Air Force members in parachutes landed in my girlfriend's tree. Some good people hid the men in a church until they could be rescued. Sometimes it was an advantage that nobody had cars; it gave people more time to do things like this without fear of being caught. My girlfriend's family cut down the parachutes from the trees, grateful for the fabric that could be sewn into something else.

My mom's uncle, Engbert Byzitter of Boerakker, Marum, is listed as one of the "ordinary (and often extraordinary) citizens of the countries occupied by the Nazis who came to the aid of Allied airmen shot down and on the run" in The National Archives (TNA) of the United Kingdom.

The Dutch Resistance movement (which we called the underground) got food for people on the black market and made false coupons. My Tante Geeske's husband, Bertus Evenhuis, was caught working for the Dutch Resistance and imprisoned at a German camp, where he stayed until the end of the war.

Building used as a safe house, Surhuisterveen

As Nazi oppression heightened, so did Dutch resistance. Hitler underestimated the Dutch, and the Nazis were unprepared to deal with the primarily non-militaristic form of resistance. Dutch intervention can further be characterized as either passive or non-violent active resistance. For example, immediately following Nazi occupation, American and British films were banned from theaters and replaced by German movies and propaganda newsreels. Dutch patrons walked out or booed during the newsreels, so laws were passed prohibiting such behavior. Subsequently, attendance at films dropped.

German radio broadcasts consisted mainly of propaganda. It was illegal to listen to British radio, but many Dutch citizens began to listen to the BBC and radio broadcasts from the Dutch government in exile. In 1943 over one million radio sets were

confiscated by Nazis in response. Radio Oranje was a Dutch radio program broadcasted from London at 9PM and read by Queen Wilhelmina for 15 minutes on the BBC European Service.

Additionally, the Dutch resisted becoming assimilated into Nazi ideals and culture. They considered themselves Dutch and looked forward to renewed independence. On Prince Bernard's birthday, many people wore orange carnations to commemorate the Dutch ruling family. German postage stamps were affixed to the upper left hand corner of envelopes since many believed the upper right hand corner was reserved for the stamp of Queen Wilhelmina.

Many Dutch citizens spoke out and published materials against the Nazis. To be caught meant imprisonment or deportation, possibly to Mauthausen, from where few returned. Clergy read letters from the pulpit. Underground newspapers flourished and were invaluable after the confiscation of radio sets and the loss of electricity during the later years of the war.

When my Tante Aukje de Boer had a baby, Grietje stayed with her family to help with chores because their maid had been called away to help with the war effort. Five onderduikers were hiding at their house. When German soldiers banged on the door late at night, the boys rushed out the back door into a hole in the field. One of the boys cried because he didn't want to be in the war.

Although coffee was scarce at this time, my aunt and uncle had a pot on the stove. They offered some to the soldiers. They must have heard the commotion of the boys rushing out but they accepted the cup of coffee, which probably was like an oasis in the wilderness. They interviewed everyone in the house, so Grietje told them why she was there. They did not look for the onderduikers.

A couple days later, a man came to our house and said to my father, "Have you got anything to do with the Germans? Some soldiers have been asking about you, so I sent them in the other direction!"

Not knowing what this was about, my dad flew on his bike to

his father's house to hide. A couple days later the same soldiers who had been to my aunt's house came to us to check out my sister's story, so there was no danger, but we had no way of knowing this. When they left, Tryntje biked to our grandfather's house to tell my dad it was okay to come home.

People in our town had to do many things in secret, and many were punished for doing the right thing. Some people hid Jews, which was more risky because the punishment was bigger if they were caught. Jews lived mostly in the city.

When the Nazis invaded Amsterdam the Jews were right away put in ghettos, so many did not have time to escape. At first Jews were given half the number of rations card as non-Jews, but pretty soon they did not get any. They sold family treasures for more rations. Some Jews escaped to the countryside because there was more food and there were more places to hide.

A church agency in our town helped find hiding places for Jews. A family from our church, the Spriensmas, hid a Jewish family in a haystack in their field. They cut a hole in it and covered the opening when the family was inside. The Germans found the Jews, and Mr. Spriensma was also taken to the concentration camp. There were four kids in the family, and the mother was pregnant with her fifth child. Mr. Spriensma never came back.

Attempts at escape from the Netherlands were rare. Countries bordering the Netherlands were under German control, so flight across the Dutch border only meant entrance into another Nazi-controlled country. The west and north borders of the Netherlands consist of North Sea coastline, and passage through German-patrolled waters was dangerous.

The Netherlands was a densely populated country. The land was flat, providing little forested, mountainous terrain suited for partisan activity or refuge. In essence, the geography of the Netherlands provided no place to run and few places to hide.

Culturally, Dutch society was stratified largely on the basis of religion. Thus, close friendships between Jews and Christians were uncommon in wartime Holland. This made it difficult for

Jews to find a place of hiding within the homes of Gentile neighbors. Most Jews who went into hiding did so individually; to go into hiding not only endangered the well-being of one's Gentile benefactors but often meant abandoning other family members including elder parents, spouses, siblings, or children.

Many Dutch citizens were deceived into believing that the Nazi occupation would not entail great hardship or the anticipated atrocities. Dutch culture and tradition reinforced the idea of obedience to the law. These two factors led many to believe that all they needed to do was outlast the German occupation. Many believed that the war would be short-lived and that, through a process of appearing cooperative and incorporating delay tactics, the impact of Nazi occupation on the Dutch, including Dutch Jews, would be negligible. Unfortunately, Nazi occupation lasted five years with devastating consequences for all of the Netherlands, including the Hunger Winter of 1945.

The winter of 1944–1945 was very harsh, which led to 'hunger journeys' and many cases of starvation (about 30,000 casualties), exhaustion, cold and disease. This winter is known as the Hongerwinter

Swedish planes dropping food provisions in Amsterdam

("hunger winter"), or Dutch famine of 1944. In response to a general railway strike ordered by the Dutch government-in-exile in expectation of a general German collapse near the end of 1944, the Germans cut off all food and fuel shipments to the western provinces, in which 4.5 million people still resided. Severe malnutrition was common and 18,000 people starved to death. Relief came at the beginning of May, 1945.

Between the time that Hitler seized power in Germany in 1933 until the end of World War II in 1945, over six million Jews were killed by the Nazi machinery. Five million other individuals *lost their lives as a result of Nazi ideology including the physically and mentally disabled, Poles, and dissidents.*

Kids in Holland had to go to school for seven years, but with the German occupation it was changed to eight years. They wanted us to be a little bit smarter I guess, so they added one more year. Gymnastics was added to our classes at this time. One of the activities was marching in rhythm – one, two, one, two – and I thought, *Okay, it's just like the Germans soldiers marching, so it must be their idea.* We usually had no fresh fruit in the wintertime, but during the war all schoolchildren got oranges and vitamins from the government. Maybe they felt sorry for people because there was not enough food.

At the end of the war there was a shortage of coal. Our church asked every family to bring some so that services could still be held in the winter. The school was no longer open all week. We would go on Tuesdays and Fridays, take our assignments home, and hand them in later. Every week we recited memory work. Our parents did not have to get after us to do our homework. We were conscientious students.

Female motorcyclists were a common sight in the 1940s.

My mother's sisters, Berendina and Fokkeline, were both nurses. They also worked as *baaksters*, or mother's helpers. Ladies in the Netherlands had to stay in bed for nine days after they had a baby, and baaksters helped them during this time. Since these women had a legitimate reason for being on the road, they were able to help with the war effort; they delivered secret messages that they hid under their clothes, and the Germans rarely stopped them. Tante Berendina had a motorcycle so she could get around quickly. She was so little, she looked like a frog when riding it. Tante Fokkeline had a Volkswagon.

Replacement tires were not available during the war because the rubber went to Germany for their trucks and tanks. When we needed a tire for our bikes we cut a strip of rubber from an old car tire and hooked it together with a metal clip. We had no inner tubes, and every time the clip hit the gravel it would make a sound, so there you went – *hoompa, hoompa, hoompa.*

We also had ration coupons for thread, fabric and yarn. Some of my cousins who were in hiding helped us by making more yarn, feeding raw wool into a machine that was operated with a pump pedal. Since girls wore dresses or skirts, even in the winter, we wore long, heavy black woolen stockings to shield against the cold. Every night we would sit around the stove to knit and darn our stockings. Sometimes we would knit things just to keep busy, taking things apart and recycling the yarn into something else.

During the war when the soles on our wooden shoes began to give away we brought them to the *klompenmaker* to be re-soled with strips of wood. When the shoes fell apart we chopped down our own trees and brought them to him so he could make new ones. The sturdiest shoes were made from oak. One pair I got during wartime was shaped so nice and very comfortable, but they did not last long because they were made from the wrong kind of wood.

On April 14, 1945, we heard that the Allies had won the war. The Germans loaded their horses and wagons, ready to flee. Some townspeople, especially onderduikers, began to fight with them. I was in the pasture and heard a gunshot; then I saw bullets shoot past. Two onderduikers were killed during the fighting – a man from our church and a police officer – as well as several others. One of our church elders was wounded, so his son made the Germans sing the Dutch national anthem. One of my classmates went to see the commotion and was shot in the arm. Having no bike, he walked home as fast as he could and was then taken by wheelchair to

Canadian infantry, Rotterdam

the hospital in Drachten, where he died because of heavy blood loss. He was 14 years old.

Canadian and American soldiers came to help us. Lots of girls liked to talk to these boys and got rides on their Jeeps, but I was only 14 and I didn't know what boys were. There were celebrations and parades everywhere you looked. That spring we planned to attend a celebration parade in Drachten, but first we had to do some fieldwork. My dad made little holes in the dirt for the potatoes. Eager for the parade, I wanted to get the job done quickly so I thought, *I'll put four or five potatoes in each hole instead of just one and we'll get lots of potatoes!* I could just as well have thrown the potatoes away, because I'm sure they could not grow in such a cramped space.

Some of the townspeople who had been forced to work for the Germans or taken to war camps did not return to us. Some who came back were very thin, and you could see on their faces that it had been a tremendous hardship. Uncle Bertus returned, all skin and bones, and told us that the Nazis had tortured him to try to make him name other Dutch Resistance workers. He could not swim, so they would hold his head under the water in a deep pool and leave him there, where he would lose consciousness. They dragged him outside the pool but made him fend for himself. Even when they tortured him, he did not share the names of his friends.

It was uplifting to be free of the presence of soldiers and to have no more fear of what might happen. It seemed that our celebrations lasted a long time and everybody had a spring in their steps.

Moving On After the War

When the war was over we got on with our lives, but we heard that many Germans were starving and suffering. The church tried to find homes for German citizens, mostly kids. Some Dutch people were not open to this because they had such hard feelings toward Germany. My boyfriend's father, a police officer during the occupation, had been killed by Nazis; his family would have nothing to do with these needy Germans. A sweet little girl named Ingrid stayed with us. We could not understand each other but we got along fine. While I was in a sewing class, I made a little brown wool coat for her.

Tryntje, Alie, and me, 1945

After the war Dad met a man at the market who lived in Zwartsluis, Overijssel. They made an agreement to swap farms, so we moved to his place. Our new neighbors had 12 kids, including a real cute little one, about two years old, with dark curly hair. We thought it was a girl. One day the kid flew down the road naked and my dad said, "Look! It is a boy!"

The older boys in this family called my sisters and me the *Friesel dames* — we had lots of attention and free helpers on our farm. A girl named Alie who lived two houses down came over and asked if she could be my friend, and ours became a close relationship.

By this time I had finished 8th grade. After 6th grade, some kids would go to the *mulo*, which was similar to high school, but most kids in the country went only through 8th grade. Boys would become farmers and girls were maids for those who could afford it. Sometimes families needed help to care for a sick or elderly family member. Families were so big that sometimes there was too much work. Women had lots of babies and were often in need of a baakster during their recovery period. Many people would say, "The de Boers have three girls, let's ask them," so we were always busy.

When I was 14 I helped a family with five little boys. The mother was pregnant and had to stay in bed, so every morning I went to their house to help where I could. The grandparents did the laundry while I concentrated on cleaning.

Although the war was over we still knitted many of our clothes, now with yarn we bought at the store. We were able to figure out many designs just by looking at them, but Tryntje and I used a pattern to knit pleated dresses with beautiful blue yarn. Tryntje's did not turn out so good, so I took it apart and knitted it for her.

For a vacation we would visit the Boonestroos, the family of the man who had been one of our onderduikers during the war. They lived by the water, so we could relax on the beach. The family grew lots of plums; they were so good, and we could eat them to our hearts' content.

Grietje, Tryntje and me

Lo and behold, the man we had swapped farms with did not like Friesland so he came back to live with us. He brought some of his livestock back to the land, so we no longer had a place for our cows. In those days workmen dug out turf from bodies of water to make strips of land for farmers. Waterways would still be on each side of the land. My dad bought some strips so our cows would have a place to go.

Sometimes the cows wanted a drink and fell in the waterways, so they had to be pulled out. Grietje was good with horses, often going to riding clubs, so she trained a horse to pull a rope to get the cows out. She checked for cows in the water twice a day. Later on, when there was a drought in the Netherlands, we let other people have cows on our land. One of these cows fell in the waterway and drowned.

In the summer Tryntje and I had the job of bringing in the cows from the field so they could be milked. There was a little lake on the way, and sometimes we would do some *pootje baajen*, or leg wading. One day we stayed too long, and there came my mother. Tryntje was closest so she got a slap in the face. I ran off, but I realized I would have to accept my punishment so I went to collect my whack, ready to run as soon as Mom's palm grazed my cheek.

Grietje was taken by bus to work at a factory in Drenthe. She did piecemeal work, putting caps on medicine bottles. Tryntje and I tried it for a little while too, but we could not get the hang of it so we found other jobs.

My dad was good with horses, which was an important skill in those days since there were no tractors. He had no fear and did so well that his brothers asked him to train their horses, too.

One day Dad went on his bike to buy some pigs. On the way home he was thinking about the pigs and not paying attention, and he crossed into the path of a car. The car hit him, and he was lucky that he just had a broken leg.

At this time I was helping my aunt and uncle. They had 12 kids and had a young couple living with them as well. I cleaned their milk cans and did their laundry and so on. I had finished for the day and was looking forward to going to a choir concert with my girlfriend. She came to tell me that my dad was in the hospital, so instead of going to the concert, I loaded the milk can onto my bike and rode 15 kilometers to milk our cows.

The broken leg did not slow my father down. One day he was training some Frisian horses to pull a wagon through a gate. He finally coaxed them through, hobbling next to them, and I thought he would get crushed in the narrow opening, but he hopped onto the wagon just in the nick of time.

Dressed in traditional
Staphorst costume

For a time I milked cows in the village of Staphorst, a village in which the people were very conservative and wore old-fashioned clothes. The women wore long black skirts and colorful vests. They wore crotchless pants underneath their skirts so they could squat during fieldwork without taking a break. Their headdresses were metal caps with lace overlays. Newborns wore white clothing for their first six weeks; after this, they wore black clothes, which looked comical to me. I would ride my bike to the farm and milk the cows with a partner so the farmers could stay in the field. Although I got paid, I was always the saving kind. I did buy a nice green raincoat and was so proud of it.

Zwartsluis, where we now lived, was also slightly more conservative than other villages. It was frowned upon to ride a bike on Sunday unless you lived a long distance from church. On Sunday nights all the young people walked through the village, looking for boys and girls. It was in this way that Grietje met a young man named Albert (Ab) Regelink in 1950, and soon they became engaged.

Ab and Grietje married on January 13, 1950, on a very cold, snowy day. A lot of relatives came to the wedding by bus and stayed late into the night. Since we had only two bed stays in our house, Grietje and her new husband stayed at a neighbor's house on their wedding night. They slept in one bed stay and the neighbor and his wife slept in the other, with only a cupboard in between, so they did not have much privacy.

Grietje was always adventurous and Ab was jolly and easygoing. The Netherlands was very crowded at that time with too many farmers, so they decided to move to North America like so many others were doing. If you wanted to go to Canada you only needed to show that you had a place to work for one year. Many Canadian farmers were eager to hire Dutch farmers because they were experienced, cheap labor. Ab and Grietje were hired by a farmer who lived close to Brampton, Ontario.

There was much ice on the North Sea this time of year, so they could not sail from the Netherlands. Instead they took a train to France and boarded a boat there. When they left for the depot my mother stayed around the corner watching them go and said, "I will never see them again." It was very hard for her.

Since we did not have a phone, the only way we could communicate with them was by airmail letters – thin, light blue paper with a red border that, when folded, had a place for the address on the other side. But we did not hear from them at first, and we found out later it was because they were having such a hard time.

The winter was harsh that year in Canada. Grietje and Ab did not know anybody else and did not speak English. Since they did not have a car, they could not even go to church. They did not want to tell us how bad it was and they couldn't say it was good, so they chose not to write at all.

One day Ab went to a granary with his boss. When Ab mentioned his place of work to a man who worked there, the man said, "You are at that farm? That is the worst place you could be. I'll come and visit you." The man kept his word and soon made arrangements for Ab and Grietje to work with the best farmer in the area, which improved their lives tremendously. They had a baby girl, Elizabeth, and Grietje began writing often.

My friends and me in Zwartsluis at a five-year anniversary celebration of the end of the war. I am at the left in the front row, reclining.

Meanwhile our family moved to a little farm in Gorredijk, Friesland, and soon after that we moved to Zevenhuizen, Groningan. My uncle told my father about a farm in Wynjeterp, Friesland, that was owned by the Kuperus family. Dad bought the farm, but we could not move right away. The Kuperus family had five boys and a girl, and their mother had cancer. The family planned to immigrate to America after she died. I did not know at the time that many years later I would marry one of the Kuperus boys.

The Kuperus family, 1951 – Back row: Hendrik (Henry), Tiete (Grace), Jon (John). Front row: Foppe (Fred), Minne (Miles), Folkert (Frank), Hinke (Harry), Albertje

Tryntje went to The Hague, the Dutch capital, to train as a nurse. From her letters we could tell that things were going well, but soon she had an inkling to also go to Canada. Grietje said she could stay with them, and Tryntje emigrated in 1951. Before she left she visited Pake de Boer, who was dying of cancer. My dad also showed the Kuperus farm to her.

Albertje Kuperus died in 1951, and the rest of the family emigrated soon thereafter. In order to immigrate to the United States you needed a sponsor, and an uncle who had immigrated to the United States sponsored the Kuperus family. He found jobs for all of them, even Pake, at different farms in New Jersey. The family stayed in a tenement house with other immigrant families until they could afford to rent a farm of their own. It was dirty and crowded, but they were in America and had hope that things would soon change.

Although immigrants were not forced to change their names, it was common practice to choose Americanized first names that sounded like one's Dutch name or at least began with the same letter.

My parents and I moved to the Kuperus home in Wynjeterp. To the left of the house was a *hutte* (hut), which held a stove, table and chairs. When workers came in from

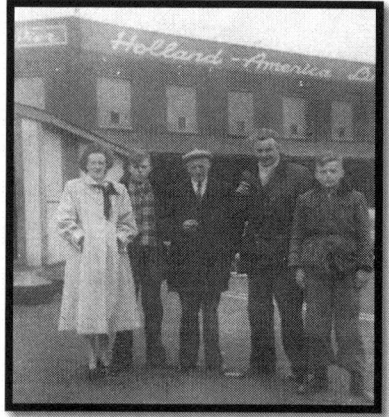

Tryntje (married to John), Folkert, Minne, Hendrik, and Harry Kuperus, 1952

the barn for the noon meal they ate here. Beyond the hutte was a milk house for equipment, and beyond that was the barn.

Another door on the other side of the hutte led to the kitchen. The left side of the house was a big living area with two bed stays. Across the hallway was a parlor, which was only used on Sunday. A stairway led to an upstairs bedroom.

Mom standing in front of the Wynjeterp house

My mother had sharp pains in her stomach for a long time. For years she went to a *boerke*, a health specialist who prescribed herbal remedies. He gave my mom a black liquid that she was to drink daily. It tasted so bad, she called it the "devil's drink." For years it seemed to help, but in 1953 the pain was so bad that an ambulance took her to the hospital.

The next day my uncle, who had a telephone, got a call from the doctor, who said that Dad should come right away. My uncle raced on his motorcycle to tell us, and Dad and I biked to the hospital. We arrived during the night and slept on stretchers in the hallway.

I had a dream that night that someone from the hospital told us we were not allowed to visit my mom, and when I woke up I was very confused, convinced it had really happened. When my dad woke up we got ready to visit Mom. Tante Fokkeline had arrived earlier, and since she was a nurse she had been able to see Mom and talk to the doctor. She said that, although my mom was strong, it didn't look good. Her gall bladder had burst and she had a blood infection. We went in to see Mom, but she could no longer talk to us. She died in the hospital.

My dad and I went to the post office and used the telephone to call Tryntje and Grietje. Mom's death came as quite a shock, so it was hard to deliver the news. My sisters could not come to the funeral since the boat ride would take three weeks and was very expensive.

The custom was to lay out the body at home. I bought a special white garment for my mom. We covered our windows with dark curtains and put her casket in the cold front room. A window was built into the casket lid so people could see her when they came to pay their respects. After four days, a horse and buggy picked her up and we went to the funeral.

After they had saved up enough money, Grietje and Ab

bought a farm in Orillia. They sent us a cute picture of Elizabeth sitting in a tub, which we proudly displayed on our mantle.

Tryntje (now called Tina) was working as a housemaid in Brampton. Soon she wrote to tell us she was engaged to Sipke (Sid) Harkema, also a Dutch immigrant. Sid, along with many young Dutch men, had immigrated to Canada because, had they stayed in the Netherlands, they would have been required to enlist in the Dutch army and serve in other countries such as India for several years. Dad prepared to go to the wedding and stay in Canada for three months. It was out of the question for me to go. The trip was very expensive, and someone had to tend to the farm.

*Wyneterp Church, where Mom and
Albertje Kuperus were buried*

At that time my uncle, recently divorced, and his 14-year-old son were living with us. Dad decided to sell his cows before he left. As a farmer, he was always easy to do something crazy. Nobody else would have made such a drastic decision, but he did things his own way. Because he did not want the field grass to grow out of control, he asked other farmers to bring their heifers and horses to our property, and it was my job to bring water buckets to the animals.

My uncle bought a little house of his own where he planned

to have chickens and other animals. There was an apple orchard on his place, and he bought a cow so it could "mow" the grass. He went to the city on his motorcycle to buy furniture for his new home, but he was in an accident and got a concussion. Another uncle came to me and said, "Jantje, he needs help, and you need to go to him. Your neighbors will have to water their own heifers." I stayed with my uncle to help him until he recovered and biked back and forth to water the livestock on our property.

My dad suggested to my boyfriend that they farm together. Since my father was such an unpredictable farmer, that did not look good to my boyfriend. It was a good thing he turned down my dad's offer, because soon after Dad left for Canada we broke up. He soon married a girl he had previously dated. We all attended the same church in Wynjeterp, which was uncomfortable.

My father's three months in Canada turned into six months. On the boat trip on the way to Canada he met a woman named Tiete. During the nine-day journey they spent a lot of time together, but they parted ways when they landed. While in Brampton, Dad reconnected with a man who had been our grocer in the Netherlands. Even in Canada, the grocer peddled his Dutch specialties from door to door because it was a convenience for so many Dutch immigrants. Dad began to go with him, and one day they stopped at the home in which Tiete was staying. It was a surprise for

them both to reconnect, and when the grocer could tell they wanted to talk more he said, "Hendrik, I'll pick you up when I am done with my deliveries."

Tiete was seven years older than dad and was the total opposite of my mother. She liked to spend money, and my mother never thought about anything for herself. Grietje tried to warn Dad, advising him to take it easy, but he did not listen and soon asked Tiete to marry him. He took her back to the Netherlands so he could sell his farm. I stayed at an uncle's house at Grietje's advice.

My cousin remarked about Tiete's appearance, saying, "She is such a beautiful lady with that blue hair!" Tiete used a rinse in her hair, and we never saw anything like that in the Netherlands. She was always dressed to the nines, and we were not used to that either.

Immigration to Canada

I saw no reason to stay alone in the Netherlands so I got my papers ready to join my family in Canada, but I needed a job in order to emigrate. Grietje had a friend in Canada who, since she was to be married, quit her housekeeping job, and I would take her place. When I got my passport picture taken I stayed with my aunt in The Hague. It was at her house that I had my first bath.

I emigrated before my dad and Tiete returned to Canada. In February of 1955 I boarded a big Seven Seas boat in Amsterdam. Passengers were assigned bunk beds, but during the daytime we mingled and had a good time. The food was out of this world. In Holland, eating an egg was a Sunday treat, but on the boat we got eggs by the plenty. When we got to the open sea the big waves rocked the boat back and forth and the eggs were "scrambled." Everyone got very sick, and the big boat was a pigsty for a few days.

Rims on the dining room tables kept the dishes from sliding off, but eventually we got used to the motion.

Every day we could see on a poster how many knots we had traveled, and we arrived in Hoboken, New Jersey, ten days later. The Statue of Liberty came into view, but those of us who were not staying in the United States did not have much time to sightsee. The boat continued to Halifax, Nova Scotia, and arrived on March 7, two days before my birthday.

We boarded a train that would take us to our different destinations. One fellow traveler, Hans, could speak English. The rest of us could not read the menu so he ordered for us, assuring us that we would like what came to the table. None of us wanted to spend much because the exchange rate was four guilders to the Canadian dollar.

Every Dutch family could take only $4000.00 when they left the country because, even though the Netherlands was too crowded, postwar conditions were poor and the officials wanted to keep as much money as they could. There was also a limit on how many family members would be accepted into the new country. Some of the Kuperuses' cousins had 12 kids in their family, but only ten could go. The others had to wait until they could afford to emigrate themselves. In later years, the government would pay people to emigrate so remaining citizens could have better housing and jobs.

I could take a very limited amount of possessions in my suitcases, mostly clothes. I was able to take some things that belonged to my mom, such as a tea light. She would light the flame inside and put a kettle on top to keep it warm. Tina had asked me to bring her some Dutch wool blankets because she was not able to find anything similar in Canada. They came in handy on the train. It was quite cold, so we wrapped ourselves up in the blankets. When the train came to Brampton, Ontario, Tina and Sid were waiting for me at the depot. They had moved in with Sid's parents, and I stayed with them until I went to work as a live-in maid for the Vokes family.

Mr. Vokes was a wealthy businessman who was known for being very kind to immigrants. He hired many people to work in his shoe factory. The Vokes home seemed like a palace with its indoor plumbing and modern appliances. So many things were new to me. Since we had no electicity in the Netherlands, I had to get used to even little things like mixers and vaccuums. We had never had an oven, so I had never baked in my life. The Vokes family had a cook, but once, when she was sick, I had to help prepare food for the guests.

Since I could not speak English at first, communication was a challenge. Once, after the Vokes family returned from a vacation, they were trying to tell me all of the exciting highlights, but I did not understand so I just smiled and nodded. I went to evening classes to learn English with other immigrants and our church services were in English, so I picked it up here and there.

The Vokes' daughter, Cynthia, was 16 at the time, and I was told that when she graduated my services would no longer be needed. The parents were very much against drinking. They thought if Cynthia were allowed to smoke cigarettes, she would not be tempted to drink, so one of my assignments was to teach her how to smoke. We would go under a tree in the back yard, and I do not know if I was a good teacher, but we had fun together. The cigarettes had no filters, and we had to always pick the tobacco from our lips. Back then we did not know that smoking caused cancer, so it seemed like harmless fun. The habit never stuck with me. It did not taste good, and I would rather save my money.

Immigration did not seem like a hardship to me. I had

cousins and friends in the Netherlands, but our family had moved around so much that maybe I was not too attached to one place. I was in a new country where the people I loved the most were also living, so that made Canada feel like home right away. We always heard that in America you would succeed if you worked hard, and I was used to that!

I made good friends right away. The church in Brampton had a very active young people's group whose members were mostly Dutch immigrants, so we had a lot in common. We met every week; the girls and boys would have separate Bible studies and then go out together. Usually we went to a restaurant where we would spend a precious dollar. We also played a lot of ping pong and had scavenger hunts twice a year. Most of the boys had cars, so we no longer went biking everywhere.

My dad and Tiete had lived in Orillia, but they bought a farm in Holland March, close to Tiete's children. While they lived in Orillia, Dad had his cows in an old shed several miles from their house, so he biked there twice a day to milk them. One morning while he was going to his cows, nine days before he was to move to his new home, he was killed when he was hit by a milk truck. The driver knew Dad and had even given him rides sometimes; he was very distraught. He said he had been blinded by the lights of an oncoming vehicle and did not see Dad. The funeral was a very sad occasion. Both our parents were gone, so it was a new existence.

When Cynthia Vokes graduated I took a job on a trial basis as a housemaid in Oshawa. The people I worked for drank like sailors. I had a boyfriend for a time but that was not going well, so I decided not to stay there.

In September of 1957 I moved in with Ab and Grietje and applied for a nursing job in a hospital. After three weeks of training, I had an interview with the hospital superintendent. He was willing to hire me, and I said I would like to visit the Netherlands at Christmastime. He told me that if I was hired he could not let me take a vacation so soon. He suggested I go right away, and I could come back to a job whenever I was ready.

I took his advice and traveled to the Netherlands, staying until January. As I prepared to return to Canada, a family friend mentioned that the Kuperus family, who now had a farm in New Jersey, was in need of a housekeeper so I applied for a three-month work permit. On the return boat trip I became very sick. I was feverish, nauseated and miserable, and I felt like I had mice in my stomach.

On the boat, before I contracted yellow fever

When I arrived in New Jersey the Kuperuses took me to a doctor, who said I had yellow fever. He suggested I take the next train to Canada to be with someone who could care for me, but I had no place to go, so he ordered me to stay inside and take it easy. At the Kuperus farm my chores were limited until I got better. I remember cooking at the stove, holding a pan with brij in one hand and a pan for throwing up in the other. The Kuperus' father helped me with sweeping the floor and setting the table.

With five boys working in the barn, there was a lot of laundry. Tryntje, John's wife, helped me with this chore. We pushed the washing machine to the sink and hooked up the hose to the faucet. After the clothes and linens were washed, they were fed into the wringer. We hung the clothes on the line outside to dry.

I applied for a three-month extension on my work permit and planned to return to Canada as a nurse's aid when that expired. On Sundays, Fred Kuperus, the second eldest son, would take me to Sussex to visit the Oukema family, whom we had known in the Netherlands, and pick me up after a few hours. Harry, the youngest son, hinted that Fred had his eye on me, but although we had nice conversations, I was not interested in him that way. Besides, it would not have been smart to date him while I worked there. If it didn't work out I would have to leave and they would have no housekeeper.

Fred Kuperus, 1955

Before I returned to Canada I requested that each of the Kuperus sons take me sightseeing to a place of their choosing. Frank and his wife Janet took me to New York City, where we visited the Empire State Building and the Statue of Liberty.

Fred had been a potato inspector in the Netherlands so he took me to a potato farm in northern New Jersey. He also took me to a beautiful farm in which cows wore a chip around their neck, and a machine that read the chip fed them just the right amount of feed. Out of the blue, Fred said he had feelings for me. I did not see that coming since he was seven years older than me. I told him I did not feel the same way, so although we did not start out on a high note, we agreed to write to one another after I returned to Canada. The Kuperus family had a farewell party for me, and on the afternoon that I left, Harry joked that Fred was hiding in the hayloft because he was lovesick.

I took a job in the hospital in Orillia and boarded with a sweet older lady that Grietje knew. I had hoped to work as a nurse's aid but was placed in central supply instead. Besides stocking medicines, one of my duties was to sharpen and sterilize needles. In those days we used the same needles over and over again. If the needle was not sharpened enough, there might be a burr left on the end, which could really hurt the patients. Gloves were also reused; if they were left too long in the autoclave, they would be roasted and fall apart.

I also assisted in the emergency room. A lot of patients had electric shock treatments. As soon as they were shocked they needed to be turned over, which took several people. Once I was called upon to comfort a wife whose husband was in a serious surgery, but I felt inadequate because I could not speak English well.

Fred and I wrote long letters back and forth, and soon he visited me in Canada. It was a 13-hour drive; he would milk the cows in the morning and then drive 500 miles to Orillia. During one of his visits there was a big fire in town, and the hospital cared for the burn victims. I asked for some time off, but it was not granted. We needed all hands for making and changing dressings, so Fred spent much of the weekend by himself. On his other trip my girlfriend had a birthday party Friday night, but Fred needed to rest after his long journey, so I went to the party while he napped. The next day we went to Wasaga Beach and other sightseeing places in Ontario. He made the trip twice, and I also visited him in New Jersey a few times. We became engaged, and sometimes I joked that we only had a few dates before we got married.

We set a wedding date but Fred had to first find a house for us. The man who leased the farm to the Kuperuses found a cute little three-bedroom house about a mile up the road from the farm.

We were married on October 15, 1960, in Orillia. From the Kuperus side, Fred's father (Pake), his housekeeper, whom we called Beppe, Frank and Janet, and Fred's sister, Grace DeVries, drove up from New Jersey. They made it a two-day trip and stayed overnight by the border in Niagara Falls, thinking they were pretty close and that the remaining drive would be short in the morning.

Pake woke up early and was after everyone else that they needed to get on the road, but the others wanted to relax over breakfast. When they got in the car they went the opposite direction,

driving 50 miles before they realized their mistake.

We had no idea what had happened to them and everyone feared that they had been in an accident, but the minister, Reverend Kuntz, said we must continue with the ceremony. Fred's family had his tuxedo in their car, but my girlfriend's brother was similar in size so Fred wore his suit and shoes. Sid and Tina chauffeured us to church in their new car. We were about a half hour late, so the guests probably wondered if there was going to be a wedding.

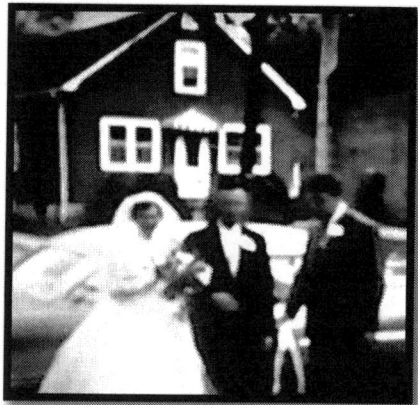

When Fred's relatives finally got to the town of Orillia they asked a policeman for directions. He said, "Follow me," and led them straight to the church, lights flashing.

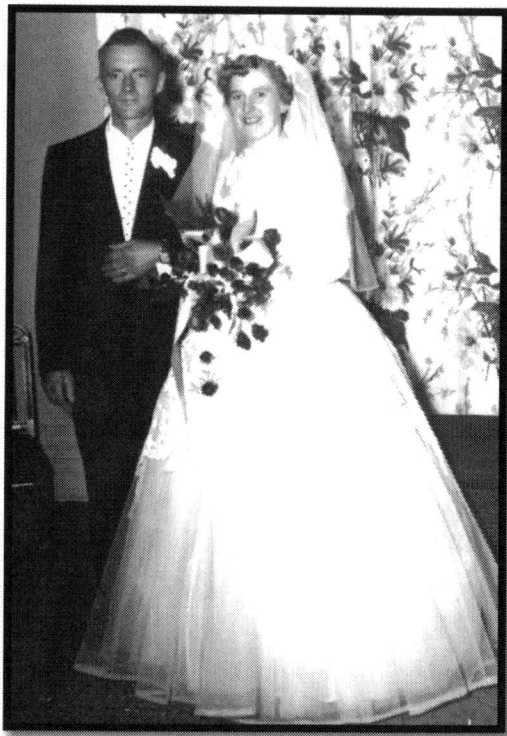

We were married in a Dutch church, and it was a tradition to have a sermon before the wedding ceremony. As the minister wrapped up the sermon he looked up and said, "Here is the family that we have been expecting." I almost cried with relief.

It was a custom for wedding guests to play a prank on the bride and groom by messing up their car in some way. Fred talked to Reverend Kuntz beforehand, who agreed that we could keep our car in his garage for safekeeping. But the man who lent Fred his suit said to the minister, "Hey, you just came from the Netherlands, and this is the way we do things here," so Reverend Kuntz handed him the keys. The young men put a "Just Married" sign on the car, using syrup to make it stick, and poured lots of extra syrup all over the car.

Most of the congregation members had attended the ceremony, and we served sandwiches and punch in the church basement. One of our gifts was a beautifully carved wooden plaque, shaped like a maple leaf. The inscription, translated, is Psalm 127:1 — *"Unless the Lord builds the house, the builders labor in vain."*

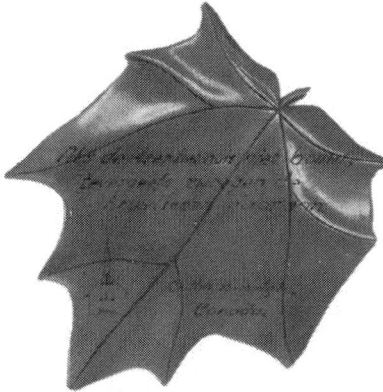

At night we had a sit-down dinner for family and close friends at a nice restaurant. Reverend Kuntz and his wife had written a nice poem about Fred and me, which was read to our guests. At the head table, Fred's father sat next to him. Ab and Grietje's little girl, Janet, always called herself "Tante Jantje's girl," and she sat right next to me. Whenever Fred and I kissed she cried because she thought Fred was hurting me.

Janet reacts to a kiss.

The plan was to leave right afterwards for our Niagara Falls honeymoon but Fred had to clean the car, so we stayed at a hotel that night in Orillia. Since we did not believe in going out to eat on Sunday, we stopped at Sid and Tina's house for lunch and then continued to Niagara Falls. We had purchased a special package for honeymooners, and a bus took us from place to place to all the sights.

At the botanical gardens we saw a giant working clock made with flowers. Fred liked to go to the museums also. I went to some,

but one time he went by himself while I stayed in the motel to write thank you cards. We bought a nice tablecloth and a plate that had a snow scene painted on it. On the way home, Fred attended the annual farmers' convention in Syracuse, New York.

A New Life in New Jersey

When we arrived in Blairstown our house was not completely ready. Janet helped us hang curtains, and the furniture that Tina helped me choose was later delivered. Our house was small, but it was so cozy. In my childhood I did not have electricity or appliances, and I could never have imagined machines that automatically washed and dried clothes. I had never baked before, so I learned to use the oven. In the Netherlands our sewing machine had a handle that had to be turned, but I now had an electric Singer machine. We bought an old black and white television set. I did not watch it much, but Fred never missed the evening news – he could not be interrupted while it was on.

Fred bought a pink car. Maybe it was cheap because of the color, but he did not mind as long as it was reliable. He gave me driving lessons, and I was relieved to pass the test and earn my license. For all the time we spent on bikes in the old country, neither of us owned one or rode one again in America. I worked two days a week for our family doctor, Dr. Baustert, earning $8.00 per day. I also did some housecleaning for other people.

Most of the Kuperus brothers worked on the family farm, down a little dirt road. I had never seen anything like this barn; it was beautiful to behold. All 100 cows had their own stanchions, which made milking a lot easier. They bought Holstein cows because this breed was closest to the cows they'd had in the Netherlands. Red Holsteins gave richer milk, but not as many pounds; they went with black and white Holsteins instead.

Extended Kuperus family, circa 1964

Many immigrants had to leave their occupations behind when they moved to the new land. They had to take whatever was available, and farming was something the Kuperuses knew they could do. I think Fred had really liked his job as a potato inspector in the Netherlands, but he never complained about farming – he was just happy to be in America. Like his brothers, he became a U.S. citizen soon after arriving. He was always interested in politics and appreciated the right to vote.

Henry was a good mechanic, so for a time he worked for a man who fixed machinery. Later he farmed on his own in the town of Sussex. Henry and Frank, both good students, would have been good teachers. Fred's youngest brother Harry, still a young teenager, lost a finger when a wagon landed on it as he was doing Sunday fieldwork. He could no longer work in the barn, and since he had not finished high school in the Netherlands, this was his opportunity. A family friend who was a veterinarian lived in Patterson, so Harry lived with him to care for the animals and earned his diploma at the same time. He then went to Calvin Seminary in Grand Rapids, Michigan, to become a minister.

In December of 1960, Tante Berendina, Sid, Tina, and their sons Frank and Henry visited us. We celebrated with a traditional Sinterklaas party. Tante Berendina always liked to make poems that rhymed for St. Nicholas Day, and her poems this year hinted about me having a baby. She could not have known, but soon after they left I was terribly sick in the mornings, and I found out I was pregnant.

Henriet Marguerite was born on August 25, 1961. Following Dutch tradition, we named her after my father (Hendrik) and mother (Grietje). We broke tradition to give her a middle name; some relatives thought this was too uppity. We tried to choose names for our kids that were more Americanized. Before we knew it, I was expecting another baby. We named our second daughter, born November 2, 1962, after Fred's mother, Albertje, and we called her Betty Ann.

My six-year-old niece Janet died of leukemia that December.

She had suffered for a long time, although Ab and Grietje had tried to spare me from the details because I was so close with her. I could not travel to her funeral with a newborn, so Fred went instead.

On the return trip the car was acting up, so when Fred came home he worked on it in our garage, which was on the basement level under the girls' room. That night Betty kept crying. I had a terrible headache and did not have enough energy to get up. Fred got out of bed but stumbled into the wall. Henriet was in the same room as the crib, but she did not wake up. We realized that the fumes from the car had probably circulated through the house, so we opened the front door wide. This probably saved our lives.

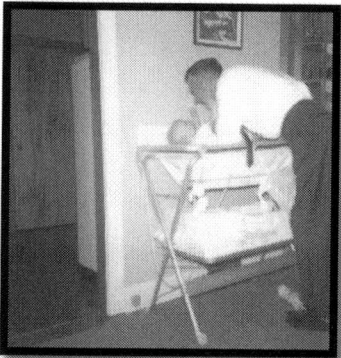

Cynthia Grace, named after Cynthia Vokes and all of the Grietjes in our lives, was born on July 7, 1964. We named our next daughter, born on February 6, 1966, Tracy Lynn, after my sister Tryntje. Miles (Mike) Fred was born on August 6, 1967.

So much was new to us in raising kids. Since I did not have my mom and my sisters were far away, my family could not give me parenting advice. Although Fred spent most of his day on the farm, he loved kids and was a good father.

Having my sisters-in-law close by was helpful, and the kids got to spend a lot of time with their cousins. When Henriet and Betty were a few years old, Frank and Janet's boys, Mark and Lee, would come to our house in the mornings.

One time the boys came over when I was still asleep. Maybe I was pregnant, because I was sleeping very deeply. The kids asked me if they could hammer some nails in the dining room wall, and I must have agreed to it. When I woke up I saw their handiwork: my china cups were hanging on a row of nails in the middle of the wall. When the girls had chicken pox, Janet brought the boys over so they could catch it, too. In those days we did not have immunizations for chicken pox, so it was good to get it out of the way when you had an opportunity.

Henriet and Betty in the play area,
wearing dresses that I knitted

We had a nice little play area with a sand box next to the house, and Fred built a fence around it. Mark and Lee and the girls were happy to have a pitcher of Koolaid, coffee or tea (with lots of milk), and played nicely for hours.

When the girls were older they walked or rode bikes to the barn almost every day in nice weather. They liked the bunnies that Ellie and Minne kept in a hutch by an outbuilding. There was a creek behind the big farmhouse in which the kids could wade and go fishing.

We attended the Newton Christian Reformed Church, along with many other Dutch immigrant families. The elders asked families to take in some kids from New York City for a few weeks in the summer so they could see what the country was like. We had some six-year-old girls at our house for a few summers. I remember Tonya as being a sweet, loving girl.

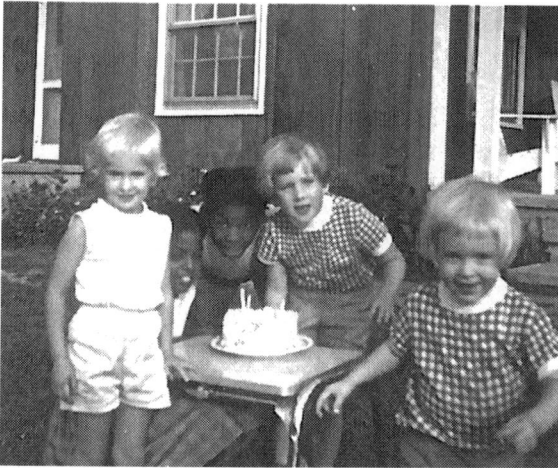

Celebrating Cynthia's's birthday with
Almeena and Tonya

We continued some traditions from the old country. We thought Christmas should be about Jesus' birth, so we gave gifts to the kids on St. Nicholas Day. I hung Christmas stockings around the dining room ceiling moulding and, starting ten days before, put a little wrapped present – a ring, a piece of candy or a little toy – in the stocking every night. The kids ran out of bed in the morning to see what had been added. They could open stocking gifts on the morning of December 6, and we hid a bigger present for later.

Fred and I gave many haircuts over the years. When the kids did not sit still the hair would be crooked, so we cut some more. When it was finally straight, there was not

much hair left. Sometimes when one of the girls went out with Fred another farmer would say, "How old is your son, Fred?"

We bought a record player and bought some Disney albums that the kids played over and over again. Sometimes they would make little books, writing stories on thin pieces of paper and sewing them together with needle and thread.

In my spare time I knitted and sewed dresses for the girls. I usually just looked at a design and copied it. I liked certain items that were only in the Netherlands, so I would mail order special yarn and clothing. When the girls were older they were not crazy about the Dutch Maid underwear from the old country.

Although I did some baking, Mr. Leinstra, a baker who had also emigrated from the Netherlands, would deliver delicacies, like a mocha-frosted cake for Sundays. I cut the maraschino cherry on top into equal pieces for the kids.

While Fred was doing fieldwork in the summertime, the kids and I would bring him a picnic lunch. We sliced strawberries and put them on bread with some sugar, which was something we used to do in the Netherlands. Other sandwich toppings were *stroop* (chocolate syrup) or *moeskes* (Dutch sprinkles), both the chocolate and rainbow varieties. From an early age the kids all loved Zoete

drops, the salty Dutch black licorice. Sometimes they would find some in Fred's Sunday suit coat pocket, covered with pipe tobacco.

The kids did not like many of the traditional Dutch foods like stampot and brij. Mike would not have survived in the Netherlands – he threw his potatoes under the table and did not like anything green. I learned to make some American foods, but Fred did not take to these, so I cooked a little of everything.

We did not lock our doors, and one night we had the surprise of our lives. I woke up 2:00 a.m. and said, "Foppe, there's somebody in the house!" I opened the door that led to the dining room and immediately smelled liquor. I looked around the corner into the living room. There, on the couch, was a man covered in blankets. I could see gray curly hair sticking out from one end; a bottle of liquor was on the floor beside the couch.

We did not wake the intruder out of fear for what he might do. I used the wall phone in the kitchen and took it around the corner into the breezeway to call the police. The policeman said he would come after another officer joined him for backup. I walked to the road to wait and flag them down while Fred stayed with the sleeping intruder.

When the police woke the man up he said, "Oh, I'm so sorry. When I left the bar, someone said I should take a right at the first light for a place to sleep." There was an inn to the left of the traffic light beyond the bar that he was speaking of. I may have left a light on in the front porch, but he was very drunk and therefore confused. He shook Fred's hand as the police led him away.

In those days hitchhikers were a common sight, and we often picked them up. One time Fred got a ticket for picking up a college girl on a busy highway. Some time after the drunkard slept on our couch, Fred picked up a hitchhiker, and it turned out to be the same man. He said his name was Curly. The next year we saw his name in the newspaper. He had been fined $25 for illegally entering another house and sleeping on their couch. We should have charged him $25 when he slept at our "inn."

Fred woke up at 4:30 a.m. for the morning milking, and I woke up with him to make his tea. Usually I would stay awake and sit at the dining room table to write letters to people in Canada or the Netherlands. One morning I heard some noises while I was at the table, but we had heifers next to our house so I didn't think anything of it. Tracy woke up and I helped her to the bathroom, which had a window looking over the back yard. Tracy pointed at the window and said, "Look Mom, a doggie!" I looked out the window and saw a man with curly hair, but I didn't want to scare Tracy so I said, "Yes, a doggie. Now you go back to sleep."

I ran to lock the doors and called the barn. Fred and his brothers came and ran around yelling, "Come out! We know you're here!" We had a garbage dump behind our house, so maybe he was hiding there. We did not find him, but after that I locked the doors for a while.

After fifteen years of leasing their farm, the Kuperus brothers wanted to buy one of their own. New Jersey property taxes were too high, so we placed an advertisement in *The Banner*, the church magazine, saying that we were interested in buying several small farms in the Midwest that were close to one another.

Sixteen people responded, and Fred and I soon went on a trip for a week to follow some leads. We went to Grant, Michigan, and Wisconsin, but nothing was just what we needed. Then Frank went to Michigan and bought a nice farm that had room for 39 cows in Coopersville. Henry followed and bought a small farm in Ravenna, which he later expanded.

Fred went to the same area to look at a farm that was for sale. It had been vacant for three years and Fred thought it looked very run down. Eventually he decided that it had potential; we bought the farm and 80 acres for $29,000.

Henry and Thea's family lived two miles south of our place. Frank and Janet lived three miles farther, and Grace and John were two miles beyond that. It was amazing how it all worked out. We all had places of our own within a 10-mile spread, just like we had hoped for.

A Move To Michigan

We moved to our new home on Heights Ravenna Road in July of 1971. Our dog Blackie rode in the moving truck cab with the driver. Mikey sat in a little seat that hooked over the front seat between Fred and me, and the four girls sat in the back of the sedan. When we came to the farm, one of the kids, I think it was Betty, said, "Do we have to live in this crummy place?" The house did look unique with its light pink siding. We had a surprise when we walked in the door: all of the carpet that had been in the house when it was for sale had been removed. We were very grateful for all the help we had from Fred's siblings and many other families from New Jersey on moving day.

The barn had separate stanchions for 40 cows. The metal roof was rusty and the wood was unpainted. The buckets from which the cows drank did not work, and the weeds were practically as tall as Fred. There was no silo on our farm, so we arranged to have one built before we arrived. Our neighbor noticed that it was tipsy, so the builders had to take it apart and start over again. Fred bought a bulk tank and other machinery. Our cows were due to arrive a week later. Fred had arranged for them to be delivered in a double-decker semi truck, but at the last minute the driver changed his mind, saying it was too far. Fred drove his pickup truck to New Jersey to find another driver. He arranged for the 40 cows to be delivered in two shipments and led the way home for the first truck.

Each of the four Kuperus siblings who had moved to Michigan had five kids, so the Coopersville Christian Reformed Church grew a lot when we joined them. The Christian school affiliated with our church did not provide busing to Ravenna. Hendrik and Thea's kids went to Trinity Lutheran School in Conklin, only 11 miles from our house, so that looked good to us. The kids were picked up by the bus, which was a luxury. It was a good thing that schoolwork was easy for all the kids since Fred and I had only gone to school through the 8th grade, and we could not have helped them.

Shortly after we moved, our well went dry. We needed drinking water for the cows, so Fred would go to a neighbor's farm to fill up water tanks that he kept on the bed of his truck. In

Deer Park Funland, Muskegon, which later became Michigan's Adventure

the meantime workmen dug for another well. They brought a lot of heavy equipment, and they charged for every foot they had to go below the ground's surface. After about a week they hit water, but this well went dry right away. This time we hired a dowser, a man who walked around with a forked stick. When he walked over a promising area, the stick would bend toward the ground. The workmen began digging again in the area he chose. We prayed and prayed, and on a Sunday morning, three weeks after the first well went dry, the workers announced success. We all joined in the "hip, hip, hoorays."

In New Jersey all the brothers had worked together on the farm, but we were on our own now. We could not afford a hired hand, so I became Fred's work partner. All of my experience in the Netherlands came in handy. Just like in New Jersey, I woke up at 4:30 a.m. to make tea. Fred had some before he went to the barn, and the rest I put in a *buske* – a small, lidded metal pail – for him to take with him, along with some butter sandwiches.

I soon followed to put the milk machines together and feed the calves. We separated the calves from their mothers soon after birth, and they were fed a milk substitute with a big bottle. Since we did not have the space to keep them, we sold them when they were old enough. If the females' mothers had been good milkers, we bought the heifers back when they were ready to calf.

We fed the cows sileage, grain and hay. Sometimes, as an extra treat, Fred would spread molasses over the hay. After the cows were fed he took a break, sitting on a cinderblock in the milk house for his tea and sandwiches. This was a tradition for the cats, too. When he sat down they all came running. One cat, which we affectionately

Twin calves were not common. These twins were even more unusual because the bull weighed 80 pounds and the heifer weighed less than 50.

called Pest, sat on his shoulder. Fred tore the crusts from the bread and they all got a little morsel. Of course they had milk to their hearts' content. The kids liked Fred to squirt it directly into the cats' mouths while he milked, but this did not work so well.

While Fred did the morning milking I returned to the house to make breakfast for the kids and get them ready for school. Their favorite breakfast was pannekoeken – I could hardly keep up with their eating. They took turns reading Bible verses while they ate. It was important to us that Bible reading and prayer were a part of every meal as it had been with our own families. I often said, "The family that prays together, stays together."

I returned to the barn for the remaining chores: cleaning the milk pails and the milk house, sweeping the hay from the troughs, and scraping the floors. When Tracy and Mike were not yet in school, they would call the barn extension and ask if they could have a treat – usually some Smarties. Our phone was on a party line in those days, shared with four neighbors. If you picked up the phone and someone from another house was talking, you had to wait until they were finished to make a call. Sometimes we needed to call the vet with an emergency and the phone would be tied up for a long time, so we would have to ask the talkers to wrap up their conversation.

Fred's last job of the morning was to load the manure into a wagon and spread it in the field. Depending on the time of year, the rest of his day (before evening milking) was filled with other chores: giving shots and pills to sick cows; resupplying stacks of hay; clipping hooves and grooming cows; restoring and fixing things, and plowing and planting crops. Fred and his brothers shared some farm equipment. In the fall, when it was time to harvest the sileage, they helped one another.

Even though people may think cows all look the same, each had its own personality. We recognized them by their markings and of course by their udders. Cows are very intelligent. When they came in from the field, most of them knew exactly which stall was theirs.

Fred thought his cows were beautiful. He spent a lot of time brushing their hides and tails and hung nameplates above each cow's stanchion. These he made himself by cutting pieces of plywood and painting them brown. Then he painted the cows' names in the center of the plates in his best fancy writing. With chalk, we wrote the date that the cow should be bred to have another calf on a corner of the plate.

The cows needed to have a calf every year in order to continue producing milk. In the Netherlands we timed the breeding so the cows would calve in the spring, but we wanted a steady supply of milk, so the breeding was staggered. We did not have bulls, so a breeder artificially inseminated the cows. Before the calves were born, the cows had to be dried off: they were not milked for a while toward the end of the pregnancy. This practice of letting them rest led to higher milk production after the calves were born.

Sometimes the cows had mastitis, an infection in their udders. They were treated with antibiotics, and their milk was to be dumped down the drain while they were taking medicine. It seemed like this came in waves – if one cow got mastitis, another would get it, and then another and another. Those were tense times.

Fred was particular about his barn, and over the years it had quite a makeover. He kept the outside freshly painted, and the inside was often sprayed with whitewash. He built a nice wooden gate around the fields and house and painted it white, with black tops on the posts.

Each cow had a drinking bowl next to her stanchion that was hooked up to the water lines. When they pushed their mouths against a lever at the bottom of the bowl, water would fill it. Every once in a while a lever would get stuck; the water would overflow and flood the troughs. Sometimes we would have to wake up the kids to bail out the water.

Although we had an electric fence, quite a few times the cows would escape. It could be a challenge to get them all back, especially when it happened at night and they got into the cornfield. One time a man drove into the ditch by our house and Fred helped pull him out. We did not know that he had crashed into our fence and made a hole in it. Later that night someone came to the door to tell us our cows were on the road, so everyone got out of bed to look for them.

On our 80 acres we grew corn for the cows, but we did not have enough land to grow all the hay we needed. Sometimes Fred put a wagon behind his truck and went all over looking for good hay. Henriet would go with him, and even before she had her license she drove back, pulling a full wagon, so Fred could have a nap.

Sometimes a load would be delivered by semi-truck, 500 bales at a time. Several people were needed on the truck to transfer bales to an angled elevator, which brought the bales to the hayloft. Here, we had an assembly line. I removed the bales from the elevator and threw them to the next person, and so on. Sometimes we used a horizontal elevator to take the bales to a different part of the loft. Fred's job was always to stack the bales. It was a terribly hot job. I kept track of how many bales we had handled and often yelled out the number to keep everyone's spirits up.

The kids all helped and were paid a penny per bale. It was

Maybe I am running away from the semi-truck full of hay?

hard work and the girls were not powerfully built but they were good workers. It was tricky to line up the 60-pound bales between the tracks on the elevator. Otherwise, the twine would break and the hay would fall to the ground. These were also tense times. One time Betty got between two bales on the elevator to get a ride to the hayloft. The chain skipped the track, pushing the bales together, but a cousin who was at the opening of the hayloft caught her just in time. Sometimes, after a long day in the hay, I would take the kids for a swim at Crockery Lake in Conklin or sometimes to Lake Michigan.

While the kids attended Sunday school after church, Fred and I got together with friends from New Jersey at someone's house. This group of eight couples, known as the "coffee drinkers," included Fred's siblings and their spouses, the Steenstras, Kapteins, Haarsmas, and Roskamps. When it was our turn to host I felt a bit intimidated because I did not have much baking experience, and the other ladies' treats always seemed better. The girls and I spent much of Saturday baking cookies, spice cakes and *zandjebakjes* (sand cakes). In December we made banket, a Dutch almond pastry. These were given as gifts to the kids' teachers and their beloved bus driver, Mrs. Beuschel.

We believed that Sunday should be a day of rest so on this day the kids could not do things like ride their bikes or swim. We had a little pond in the field, and when it froze in the winter the kids would skate on it. One Sunday Cynthia and her cousin, Amy, asked Fred if they could skate and he said yes (I would have said no), and they fell through. Another time I found Betty, Cindy and Tracy hiding in a bedroom, where Betty was teaching her sisters how to knit. Knitting was considered work in the Netherlands, so this was against our rules. For a while the kids could not even do homework on Sundays, but this changed when they were in high school.

On Mondays after school, the kids went to catechism classes at church. Our new minister asked me to teach a class. The kids started out singing hymns, so I would play the few I knew on the organ, and then we would meet for classwork. The kids could be a handful. When the previous pastor's wife taught, she threatened to kiss the boys when they misbehaved. My strategy was to offer a candy when kids did their lesson, but I got the feeling that one of the church elders disapproved when I told him about it. One week I wore a jacket I had just sewn, made of red and white polyester checks, and one of the boys in Cynthia's class showed up with a leisure suit made of the same material.

I continued to make clothes for the girls as well: pantsuits, vests, and dresses, usually with polyester fabric. I preferred "friendly" patterns. I did not like to throw remnants away, so for one Christmas I made each of the kids a quilt sewn out of fabric scraps. They could look at it and remember our outfits through the years. Although the kids tried to persuade Fred to wear jeans, he always wore the same dark green work pants and usually a plaid shirt, unbuttoned too much.

As farmers, we were at the mercy of the weather. If it rained too much, the ground was like a sponge and the tractor would sink in the ground. If there was no rain and the corn did not grow, we had to buy sileage from someone else. One time the cows would not eat the sileage we bought, and it turned out to be moldy so we had to throw it away.

One year the ground was quite wet, but the equipment was not sinking, so Mark (Frank's oldest by) and Henriet were each on a tractor, pulling the harvester together. The tractors were both attached to the harvester with chains. The chain behind Henriet's tractor snapped off and hit her on the shoulder. She was very sore, but we were lucky she was not hurt more.

The sump pump in the house stopped working when the power went out for many days due to severe rainstorms. There was a foot of water in the basement and if it rose any higher it would reach the furnace, which would not be good. We set up an assembly line to bail out the water.

Winters brought other challenges. Everyone helped shovel two tracks in the driveway so the cars and milk truck could get through. The snow mountains were so high at the end of the driveway that someone had to stand there and wave drivers out when it was safe to go. One time nobody else was home and I had to pick up the kids, so I took a chance and flew out of the driveway when it looked safe from one direction, but I kept thinking later how unwise this was.

We had a tremendous ice storm in 1978. The ice on the trees was so heavy that huge branches snapped off. Most people lost power for a long time but we were spared for the most part, so lots of kids (20 at one time) came to our house to stay warm. Henry was one who lost power for many days in a row. His cows bawled like crazy because it was so painful when they were not milked on time, and he borrowed our generator.

In 1981 we had terrific snowstorms four weeks in a row. The kids watched Channel 8 every morning to listen for the school closings, listed or read alphabetically by weatherman Craig James. We could not keep up with the shoveling, and the milk truck could not get through. Fred stored the milk in the cows' water troughs, but these were rusty and the milk was not sterile, so this milk was picked up and used to make dog food.

Fred planted lots of trees and added an outbuilding to the right of the barn for more storage. Between the barn and the house were his workroom, a garage and a little section that the kids turned into a playhouse. Many times photographers would fly over the farms and take pictures; then they went door to door to sell them.

Our kids matched up great with Henry and Thea's kids. They biked back and forth to each other's homes all the time in the summer. Henry had a manmade pond on his property and the kids went swimming in it, even though it was covered in clouds of mosquitos. Once they noticed that Henry and Thea's youngest boy, Johnnie, was missing, so they linked arms and walked across the whole pond, thinking he could have drowned, but still no Johnnie. They later found him sitting under a tree reading a comic book.

Mikey and his cousin Frankie

The kids were big readers, so they biked the two miles to the Ravenna library all the time. When they played baseball and softball in Little League they biked to practices and games. I came to watch when I was done with barn chores, but Fred came only once to one of Mikey's games because he could not get away from milking. While we sat on the bleachers I pointed out the batter, the son of family friends. Fred said, "Is he the boy with the stick?" Although he watched the Olympics, he did not think much of other sports, thinking grown men should have better things to do than chase a ball. He never had the luxury himself of playing games or having a hobby – there was always work to be done.

Fred had a hard time leaving the milking to someone else. We took one vacation to Mackinaw Island. Some years we would rent a little cabin at the Christian Reformed Conference Grounds in Grand Haven, and Fred would come occasionally after milking.

We lived very simply. Farming was unpredictable and we never knew what would come around the corner, so it was better to keep the money in the bank instead of spending it. The kids each got $5.00 for birthdays, and we celebrated by going to McDonalds, where each person could spend $1.00. We took the kids to two movies: *The Hiding Place* (1975), the story of Corrie ten Boom, a Dutch woman whose family hid Jews and was sent to a concentration camp; and *In Search of Noah's Ark* (1976).

Thea introduced us to her great discovery: the Ravenna Flea Market. Every Monday morning vendors would come and sell all kinds of treasures. The kids could each spend a quarter; Mike bought *Richie Rich* comic books and stuffed animals and the girls bought clothes and trinkets. Once there was a box of white kittens for free, so we said we would like to take them home to our farm. The owner said, "To a barn? No way!" so we went home empty handed.

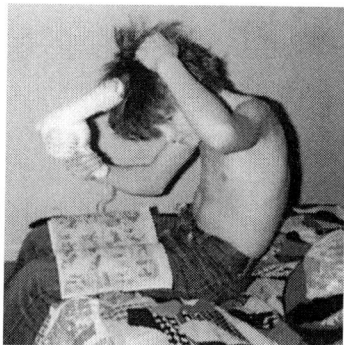

Later in the day there was a livestock sale, and Fred would go occasionally. One day some boys were selling a little black foal for $3.00, and the kids wanted it badly so we bought it. The boys put the foal in the back seat of their car and delivered it to our house for another $2.00. When the kids tried to feed the foal (which they named Midnight) with a bottle, it did not work so well. It needed its mother.

Fred called the owner and bought the mother, a white mare that the kids named Galaxy. We kept them in an outbuilding that we called the Hansel and Gretel house. We told the kids not to try to ride Galaxy since we did not have a saddle, but they did not listen. When Frank and Janet's kids were over, Tracy was showing off a little, and Galaxy backed her into a corner and kicked her knee. I found her crying outside. She did not dare tell us at first what happened because she had disobeyed. Not too long afterwards, we sold the horses.

We always had a pet dog, but many of them had short lives. Over the years we had Blackie, Smokie, Cadbury, Cyrano, Confucius, Prince, Digger, Wally, Malachi, Shaggy and Rochester Boswell. The road we lived on could be busy, and many dogs had bad habits like chasing cars and wandering to other farms. One time a

Tracy and Mike with Cyrano

neighbor physically abused our dog when he wandered to the neighbor's property, maybe looking for a girlfriend. We took the dog to the vet for corrective surgery. When we watched the evening news we had a surprise. As we watched a report about how vets were experimenting with acupuncture on animals, there was Digger on the TV screen with needles all over. We had not been asked if he could be a model and were not paid for his contribution to science.

When a dog died, usually from a farm accident, Tracy would cry for one hour exactly and then take out the newspaper to look at the "Free to good home" section. Maybe we were not such a good home, but nobody ever turned us down.

We had lots of cats to catch the mice – at one time we had 17. The mothers always had their litters in the hayloft, and sometimes they hid them deep into the layers of the bales. These kittens would end up quite wild if we did not find them in time.

When the kids turned ten years old they began to take turns with the evening milking. They fed the calves, washed the cows' udders before they were milked, swept the hay, scraped the floors and washed the milking equipment afterwards. They earned a quarter for each turn in the barn and also earned money by picking strawberries and blueberries. During the school year they picked

apples at the Sparta orchards to earn money for an 8th grade trip to Chicago. Most of the money they earned went into the bank, but sometimes they bought something special, like a cassette tape recorder, which was new in the 1970s. From the time the girls were about 12 years old, they babysat. Earning a quarter an hour was much better than a quarter for a whole evening in the barn.

Jobs in the country were not glamorous, but the kids took what they could get to earn money for college. Henriet and Betty worked in a nursing home in Marne. The girls had factory jobs in the summers. Betty and Cynthia were full service gas station attendants at Lemmen Shell station, which only hired girls for this position. Betty became a milk tester with Dairy Herd Improvement Association. Betty and Cindy packed meat in their Uncle John's butcher shop. Mike worked for Swanson Pickle Company in Ravenna, starting out as a pickle picker and then building docks and getting pickle tanks ready for brine. We always had reports that the kids were hard workers.

I also began earning a paycheck in 1980. Thea had been working as a demo lady at grocery stores, giving food samples and coupons to customers. She got me a job, and I loved it. I always appreciated a bargain myself, and I think the customers could see I was excited to pass along a good deal.

Fred had some mishaps through the years. He rolled with a tractor into a ditch and miraculously did not have even a scratch. While working on the silo unloader at the very top he lost his footing. He could have fallen to the bottom, but was able to grab on to something and regain his balance. He broke his leg when a cow stepped on it. But he was spared serious injury, as were the kids.

The kids had to entertain themselves, and we did not always know what they were up to since we were so busy working. They would jump from the rafters in the hayloft into piles of straw, and one time when Betty was fluffing up the straw Tracy jumped at the same time and got a jab in her head with the pitchfork. Mike would fly all over on his ATV, usually with Dig riding in front, ears flapping

in the wind. Sometimes he hooked a saucer sled to the back and flew the kids around the house as fast as he could. The kids mowed the lawn (maybe they were too young), and one day Cindy was going to use a tool to clean the mower blade. The mower was still running, and I yelled through the window to make her stop. When the kids tried to ride even the most gentle cows (like a cow whose blind eye stuck out three inches, whom we named Blindie), it did not work so well.

Lots of kids meant lots of cars, and sometimes the good deals turned into bad cars. The girls drove the silver Maverick to school, about an hour away in Hudsonville, but it had no heat, a hole in the floor covered with cardboard, and leaked fluid inside. Our blue station wagon, "the Bomb," was not a favorite, either. Other lemons were the boxy brown Aspen, the 4-door red Nova and the "Federal car" – a hand-me-down from the police. All these cars were broken in and often breaking down. Once, two of the cars had a "meeting" on the same day.

We had a tradition to go bowling on holidays with relatives. You never knew where the ball would end up, sometimes in the next lane or behind us. One time Fred got three strikes in a row and the kids said, "Dad, you got a turkey!" He asked, "Where do I pick it up?"

Fred and I celebrated our 25th wedding anniversary with a party at church. My sister-in-law Janet, a marvelous cook, helped with much of the food, and the men dressed up like women to serve.

One by one the kids left for college. It was assumed that they would go to Calvin College in Grand Rapids; we did not know of other options. They were on their own to figure out how it all worked, since we had only been through 8th grade. Henriet, in her experience at the nursing home, found that she was good at taking care of people and went into nursing. She would later become a great help to us with her medical knowledge. Betty used to help Fred with his farm records (we had no calculator) and liked an accounting class in high school, so she became a CPA. When Cindy was very little she bribed her siblings to play school, even asking for schoolbooks when it was her birthday. Her 5th grade teacher, Mrs. Roman, wrote on her report card that she was a natural teacher, and that was what she became. Tracy was a very serious student. Her involvement in high school debate made her interested in politics, so she majored in political science and became a Calvin professor. If Mike had enjoyed farming he would have inherited the farm, but he had no interest. He majored in business and became the manager in a furniture factory.

In the 1980s farmers were producing too much milk, so we received fewer and fewer dollars per pound. We heard of a program in which the government would buy a farmer's herd if he agreed to stop producing milk and butcher his cows over a period of 6-18 months. Not everyone would be chosen; each farmer could place three bids, and the government would only accept so many. The bid was in terms of dollars per hundredweight of produced milk.

When President Carter entered into office in 1976, he worked toward fulfilling his promise of higher milk prices. Congress passed The Food and Agriculture Act of 1977 as a vehicle to increase prices for the next several years. However, policy makers did not anticipate corresponding increases in milk supply. In 1981 legislators were faced with two choices: to reduce the support price and thereby discourage production, or continue to support milk production but reduce the surplus by other means.

After an attempt to adjust support prices did not result in the anticipated decrease in supply, assessments were collected from farmers to discourage oversupply. Farmers who reduced the amount of milk marketed received direct payments. The Food Security Act of 1985 included the provision of a whole herd buyout program. Under the Dairy Termination Program (DTP), farmers who participated in the buyout agreed to refrain from dairy farming for the next five years. Cows and heifers that were owned by participating farmers were to be exported or slaughtered. Participation was voluntary. Interested farmers submitted sealed bids for the minimum price per hundredweight that they would accept in order to comply. Out of the nearly 40,000 bids submitted countrywide, 14,000 were accepted.

One man who had Jersey cows was eager to get out of farming and only bid $4 per hundredweight. His bid was accepted, but he did not get much money. Our bid of $22.50 per hundredweight was accepted. We opted to phase out our herd in 18 months, which gave us time to use our hay and feed supplies. We had many cows that gave a lot of milk – one cow gave 100 pounds of milk per day – so we were happy to be able to continue for a while. The cows in the buyout program were branded so they could not be sold to nonparticipating farmers. Our herd slowly decreased. When a cow went dry, i.e., stopped producing milk, it was butchered.

From *The Ravenna Independent*, May 1986:

Dairy-herd Bids Accepted

Whole-herd buyout results:

Secretary of Agriculture Richard Lyng decided that $22.50 was a reasonable bid. The following are the program highlights.

The Secretary took a maximum $22.50 bid. The producer making more than one bid will have his LOWEST bid accepted. For those producers having bids accepted, they must specify their payment option before April 18, 1986.

PLEASE CONSIDER THE TAX CONSEQUENCES BEFORE DECIDING.

Michigan had 1,945 farmers make 5.212 bids. About 37% of Michigan dairy farmers bid in the program.

Michigan had 846 BIDS ACCEPTED (approximately 13.4% of farms.) The average bid for Michigan was $15.24. The bids amount to 638 million pounds of milk or 11.67% of 1985 production. A total of 46,146 cows; 22,565 heifers; and 14,332 calves were on contract farms.

National totals were as follows: 13,988 farms were accepted with 12.28 billion pounds of 1985 marketings. Average bid was $14.88. This was 8.8% of 1985 U.S. milk supply. A total of 1,550,403 head of cattle. The magnitude of this program is just now becoming apparent.

Fred's leg had begun to bother him in the fall of 1986. He felt like he had no circulation and would often soak his leg in hot water. The doctor said that the femoral artery in his thigh was blocked, and surgery was scheduled.

When we arrived at the hospital Fred was first taken upstairs to have his carotid arteries checked. If those were blocked, there was a risk of stroke. Sure enough, when he came downstairs, the doctors said he had to have that operation first; the leg surgery would be done five days later. Both surgeries went well. When our pastor visited Fred in the hospital he mentioned that he hoped to go to Israel in the fall of 1987 and Fred said he would like to go, too. The pastor told me he didn't think Fred would be ready.

A hospital bed was set up for Fred in the front room by the big picture window. During his recovery he did not ask how things were going on the farm and never set foot in the barn until April, choosing to leave all the worries behind. We hired someone to milk our remaining 17 cows, and Mike and I helped out as much as we could. We had a good neighbor in Ike Helsen; he was always willing to help and give advice. Spring came early that year and one day it got too warm in the barn. The vet said that I should open the windows, because if one cow got pneumonia, they would all get sick. If this happened, we would have to give all the cows medication and throw the milk away. I asked the vet to go in the house and explain things to Fred so he could have the final word on some decisions.

Fred recovered slowly but surely, and our Israel trip was planned for September 19, 1987. One day in late August during the morning milking I said to him, "Shall we ship the cows tonight and sell them at the Monday sale?"

Fred said, "What are you talking about?"

I explained that if we sold the cows we could invest the money before the trip. Fred said, "Good idea. Let's do it." We called the man in charge of the sale, and the cows were taken that night. During all the years we lived in Ravenna, we never locked the doors – we didn't even have a key. The kids said we should lock up while we were on such a big trip, so we had a key made.

Fred's sister Grace also went to the Holy Land with us. We went to the Netherlands first to visit relatives and go to the towns in which we had lived. In the Holy Land we were in a tour group with a very knowledgeable guide who explained what we would be seeing

at every stop, and then we could walk around to explore the site on our own until it was time to board the bus. If Fred had in his mind to see something he could become very determined, pulling on the skin under his chin in concentration. I did not always go with him in times like this, and he was often the last to board.

In Bethlehem, besides visiting the places that Jesus had walked, we went to a cemetery that planted trees to commemorate people who had helped Jews during World War II. We heard that a tree was there for a man from Zwartsluis named John Post, a farmer who had worked in the Dutch Resistance. We had both known the family. Fred found this tree eventually, on his own, but the bus had to wait for him.

When we returned from our trip we sold the farm. It turned out to be good timing; the kids were in college, getting married or moving away, so we had no kids at home to help with haying and other chores. The buyer said we could stay in the house for a while, so we could take our time sorting our belongings. On the farm we burned many things in the fire pit behind the barn. Sometimes it was hard to know what to keep after all those years. I asked Fred what I should do with my wedding dress and he said, "You will not wear it again, so add it to the heap!" The kids were not happy when they heard about this.

Some of our good friends who had also participated in the buyout program bought a house in Jenison. When we visited them we saw a house on Roselane with a "For Sale" sign in the yard. The owners showed us around and it looked good, so we bought it. Every move we made was an improvement, and this was also the case when we moved to Jenison.

Retirement and An Empty Nest

Watching my beloved Detroit Tigers, 1988

Since we did not have the farm anymore to keep us busy, we found new things. People have asked me if it was a big relief to be free of the early waking and constant work, but it had not seemed like a burden.

Sometimes when people retire they do everything together, but Fred and I each did our own things for the most part. Fred liked it when I worked at my demo job because he had the house to himself. I also did some volunteering and babysat our grandkids. We had been blessed with five healthy kids but when they were growing up we did not have time for much play. It was different with grandkids. When they were born I was able to spend time with each of them and help the families.

What Fred loved most about retirement was his volunteer work. One day a week he went with friends to volunteer at

101

International Aid. Another day every week he graded lessons that inmates had completed through Prison Ministry. He picked up food from restaurants all over and brought it to Mel Trotter. If men came to the food kitchen they had to listen to the sermon first, and Fred joined them.

On Thursday nights we both went to East Ottawa Special Ministry. Most people, including me, were assigned to one person with a disability. We had a Bible lesson and became friends. Fred met with the severely mentally impaired. They could not do a lesson, so he just talked and laughed with them and gave them hugs. He also delivered Meals on Wheels. Once the police stopped him when he was speeding, but Fred convinced the police that these people needed their food right away, so the police let him go.

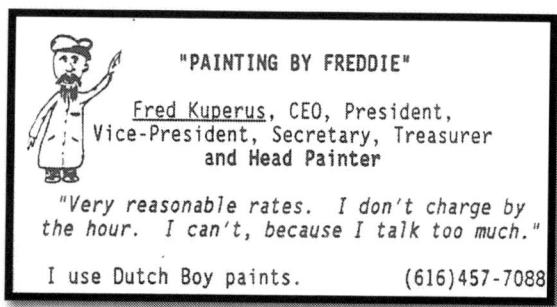

"PAINTING BY FREDDIE"

Fred Kuperus, CEO, President, Vice-President, Secretary, Treasurer and Head Painter

"Very reasonable rates. I don't charge by the hour. I can't, because I talk too much."

I use Dutch Boy paints.   (616)457-7088

The kids made this business card for Fred.

Just as Fred had enjoyed painting on his farm, he now enjoyed painting for other people. One of his jobs was in Grand Rapids. He loaded up the truck with his ladder and supplies, but when he got to the house, his ladder was gone. He must have left the lift gate open, and it fell out on the road. When he backtracked, he found that someone had put it on the side of the road.

Hurricane Hugo hit South Carolina on September 24, 1989, and we traveled two days later with a group through the Christian Reformed World Relief Committee. Two other couples from our church went as well, and we stayed for three weeks. We did all kinds of things to fix up homes that had been damaged: roofing, painting and repairing. One little old lady whose house we fixed had only two teeth. She was so thankful. We were all from different places, but were like-minded and had such good camaraderie. At the "Last Nail Ceremony" we sang, "To God be the glory, great things He has done!"

I became a citizen of the United States of America in 1993. Even though I had married Fred, who was a citizen, I was still considered a resident alien. I needed to go once in a while to renew my papers to the USCIS (United States Citizen and Immigration Services) office in Grand Rapids. However, that office was going to close, and in the future I would need to go to the Detroit office which would have been very inconvenient. After I passed the written test I attended a ceremony in Grand Rapids, accompanied by Fred and Henriet.

Cape of Good Hope, 1993

Fred and Cindy visited Tracy and Matt in South Africa in 1993. I was happy to stay home, but I later heard many stories about Fred's antics. He would do his own personal sightseeing whenever he wanted, not telling the kids where he was going. It was like the kids were his parents and he was the naughty boy. One time Fred opted not to go on a safari – he wanted to see elephants but this place could not guarantee an elephant sighting – so when the kids left they made sure all the windows and doors of the house were locked. When they came home Fred met them outside and said, "You can't keep a lion in his cage!"

Fred and I went out West with Cindy and Tracy in 1994. Fred was never shy about striking up a conversation with strangers. At the

Black Hills, our motel was on an overlook and many benches were spread around the parking lot so guests could enjoy the view. Fred would go often to smoke his pipe and enjoy the beauty. One night only one bench was occupied by a couple who was enjoying the view and a private conversation. They were far away across the parking lot, and instead of choosing any of the empty benches close to us, Fred joined them.

In August 1995 Fred went to Russia with a group from Josh McDowell Ministries, but I, being more of a homebody, chose to stay home. Fred was always interested not only in American politics, but in learning about how other countries were run. To prepare for the trip Fred read many books about Russian history and learned how the people had suffered under terrible rulers. They did not have religious freedom, and he considered sharing God's Word a necessity and a great privilege.

Because they were staying in some questionable areas and could not speak Russian, the group was told during orientation that they should not wander by themselves, but Fred disobeyed. While he was giving a Bible and literature to a man at a bus station, someone slammed the man forcefully into the wall and began to hit him. A police was there to intervene, but I think it scared Fred into staying with the group for the rest of the trip. He lost his hearing aid in a bathroom, and it's a wonder that he found it when he went back.

When Fred came back he wrote a piece for the church newsletter, referring to Russia as "that great harvest field for the gospel." He closed by saying, "What a

Giving Reeboks to kids at a Russian orphanage

contrast it is coming back to America with all its bountiful blessings. As an immigrant, I have loved this country from the first day that we set foot on its soil – now 45 years ago in Hoboken, New Jersey. This country gave me and my family a name and a place in which to live the American Dream in a small way."

Losing his "attachments" became a habit for Fred. We went to a restaurant soon after he got his dentures and they were uncomfortable so he took them out, wrapped them in a napkin and put them next to his plate. When we got home he realized that he had left them at the restaurant. Luckily, the busboy noticed the dentures and put them aside, but it must have been quite a shock for him to see someone's teeth on the table.

Fred visited his cousin in Dorr and they had a long conversation under a tree. When he came home he said that on the drive home he could not see very good, and he realized that one of his lenses had popped out. He went back to his cousin's house and looked under the tree. Since he had been there, someone had ridden over the area with a tractor, and there were tire tracks all over the ground, but he found his lens – covered with dirt, but without a scratch.

We got together with the Kuperus siblings and their spouses for birthdays, and on holidays we would go to parades and mini-golfing. Maybe the people behind us would get some big laughs, but we had fun. The Kuperus women began a long-standing tradition of meeting for lunch once a month. I was introduced to Chinese food this way. I did not know what I was missing all those years.

Fred still did not like to experiment with foods – I continued to make him brij, Dutch oxtail soup, and of course potatoes every day. I went to the Dutch import store often for windmill cookies and King peppermints.

When Mike and Betty's daughter Rachel was born in February 1996, I went to their house in Alabama for two weeks. Fred would join us for the second week. Before I left I finally taught Fred how to make potatoes. He tried it once and went out to eat every day after that.

Fred was feeling tired and sometimes light headed so we suggested that when he landed in the Tennessee airport, he should get a ride on an airport taxi from the terminal to the baggage claim area, where we would pick him up. There he came, being pushed in a wheelchair by a petite girl! He had not seen a taxi and happened to see the wheelchair instead, so this seemed like a good idea according to him.

When we returned home Fred saw a doctor. He was sent to the hospital for a treadmill test, and after some more testing we learned that his left kidney had failed, which led to congestive heart failure. He had a silent heart attack in April. In the hospital he had a dream in which he arrived at heaven's gate and asked to come in. He heard a voice telling him to return to the world because he still had work to do. In May, when he was given six months to live, the kids all came home.

A wonderful hospice nurse came for a couple of months to check him and give suggestions. Slowly he regained his strength and he no longer needed hospice. He continued his volunteer work and felt good enough to travel again. Fred wrote for the church newsletter, saying, "Looking back at my lifetime, I do not see myself as a leader, a writer, or an orator. I am just a simple ordinary person; just a servant to the lonely, the helpless, and the downtrodden. I love life, seeing it as God's gift to us all."

In April of 1997 we went by train to visit Tracy and Matt in Boston with Cindy, Betty and Josh, Betty's oldest boy. One day it was so warm, we went to the beach; the next day we had 24 inches of snow. The girls and Josh stayed in the house in which Tracy rented some rooms from a couple, and the power went out. The couple had told Tracy ahead of time that they would be gone that weekend, so she went into the main area of the house to get some candles or flashlights. But the woman had decided to stay home and went to bed early. She had a rude awakening when Tracy opened the hall closet. Compared to the others, Fred and I were in luxury in our heated motel room. Fred and Josh had a sleeper car on the train so Fred could rest better on the long trip home.

The rest of that year Fred continued to volunteer and enjoyed mostly good days, but in March he got worse. He was always so tired and did not have much of an appetite, but he was never in pain. In his last weeks somebody gave him a tape of Dutch hymns, and he loved to listen to these. It was well with his soul, and he was ready to go. He died on April 2, 1998. He had prepared his own funeral service, insisting that it be a celebration instead of a time of mourning, and the ministers and other staff at Baldwin Street Church made sure that was the case.

Life has always been good to me. I have always had more than I needed and never lacked for anything. Even in times of poor health and difficult circumstances we took it in stride because we knew we were in God's hands. Although I was now alone, I had so much to be thankful for. Fred and I had been married for 38 years and since we saw things the same way we had a good marriage. As before in my life when there was a big change, I knew I needed to keep going.

Henriet took me every summer to Canada to see my sisters and their families. We also visited the pastor who married Fred and me (Reverend Kuntz) and his wife and my girlfriends. Grietje and Ab had raised their three children in Orillia. They had some cows, and Ab worked as a cattle dealer. Grietje continued to love animals, especially horses. She had rooms full of ribbons and trophies that her horses had won at shows all over the United States and Canada. Their doors were always open to their many friends.

Tina and Sid raised their seven kids in Brampton. Sid had a successful business called Harkema Trucking Line. Tina was such a devoted mother and so gentle, kind and humble. She was very involved in her church with Bible studies and outreach.

The de Boer family had a reunion in the Netherlands in 2008, and Henriet went with me. Grietje and her oldest daughter, Elizabeth, also went. It was enjoyable to catch up with relatives and see all the buildings that had been a part of my childhood. Henriet and I went to all seven homes in which our family had lived. We knocked on the doors, and most of the new owners let us in to look around. Many of the homes are still operating as farms, although at the Wyneterp property the owners built a house separate from the barn. The house in Zwartsluis had been taken down when the waterway was expanded to make room for bigger ships.

A couple of times the kids and grandkids took me back to the Ravenna farm. Although the land was still being used for crops, there were never again cows in the barn. I could not resist picking up a broom, still leaning against a wall, and sweeping the floor for old times' sake. The nameplates that Fred had painted were still hanging, so we asked the new owner if we could take them for memorabilia. We had named cows

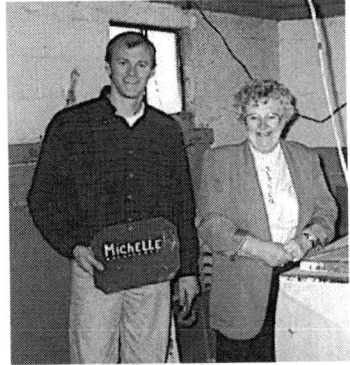

If Mike had been a girl he would have been Michelle.

after all of the kids, so they tried to find the plates with their names.

For many years I have visited people in nursing homes, especially those who are not able to go to church anymore. I might bring a roll of King peppermints and play a game. My game of choice used to be Scrabble, and I would often play against myself at home, but now I prefer dominos and Upwords.

My 80th birthday celebration

I had such a surprise in the fall of 2014. Tonya, one of the girls from New York City who had stayed at our home in New Jersey, called me. She had been in New Jersey the summer before and had driven past a mailbox with the Kuperus name on it. She stopped not only there, but at two other Kuperus homes to track me down. She came to visit me with her husband, and I was amazed at the vivid memories she had of her time with us. She remembered that I allowed her as a seven year old to walk a mile down the dirt road to the barn. Tonya and her husband have a son at Princeton, and she turned out to be a successful, vibrant woman. It made me realize that you never know the influence you may have on someone's life.

I have always enjoyed my independence, and I have been blessed with the strength to do whatever has been necessary, but it was time to start thinking about selling the house. Henriet helped me sign up at Sunset Manor in Jenison, and a room would be waiting for me when I was ready.

In June of 2015 I was trimming the hedges with an electric clipper and nearly chopped off the top of my finger. I went in the house to call Tracy, wrapped up the finger with towels, and went outside to finish the job until Tracy arrived to take me to the hospital. A hand surgeon was able to fix the finger, but it seemed like a good time to move.

I retired in 2015 after 35 years of service.

It was good that I had so many kids, because it took everyone to make the big move. Cindy came from New Jersey and spent a few weeks starting the big project of figuring out what to do with 84

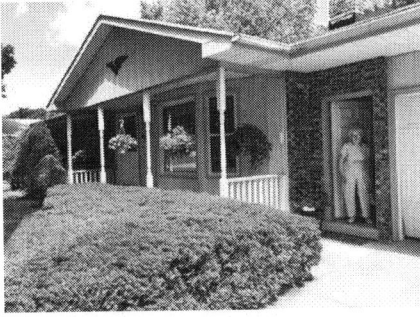

years of possessions. It was sometimes challenging to figure out what to do with everything – it has always been hard for me to part with things, because some day you might miss it. My niece Amy helped the kids with a garage sale. Kuperus Trucking delivered many things to a mission in Mississippi. With all of that help, the transition to Sunset in September of 2015 was very easy.

I live in luxury here at Sunset, like a princess in a palace. I have become fast friends with my tablemates during mealtimes, and the food is out of this world. I may feel like royalty, but I have to be careful or soon I will be queen-sized. The staff is so nice and helpful and with all the activities, nobody can be bored. We are fully entertained with choir and symphony performances, movies, magic shows, cooking classes, Wii, lots of games, and Bible studies. The Hoekstras take me to my church, and there are also chapel services at Sunset.

My grandkids are growing, and many live far away. They are involved in things that sound interesting, but sometimes it is beyond my understanding! I wish my kids and grandkids all the best and want them to know that I love each and every one of them. God's promises are available to all who seek Him, and it is my hope that they will love the Lord and follow in His ways.

Afterword

The Kuperus family took in many onderduikers during the war. A friend who owned a clothing store was involved in the Dutch Resistance, and when the Germans discovered his activities he hid at the Kuperus farm, bringing new coveralls for the boys.

Minne and Albertje Kuperus, 1951

A hill in the back of the field presented a good hiding place for onderduikers. The men hollowed it out and lined it with straw. The two older Kuperus boys, John and Foppe, slept here with the onderduikers until it became too cold. Although they had Ausweises themselves, there was still reason to fear the Germans.

One Saturday night in 1944 German soldiers came to the Kuperus home and shouted one word over and over: "Weapons! Weapons!" Although the family claimed to have none, the soldiers grabbed the father, Minne, and oldest brother, John. German records showed that another son over 18 years of age by the name of Foppe had been issued an Ausweis, but he was nowhere to be found. After a fruitless search of the home the soldiers left, taking Minne and John with them to a villa in Beetsterzwaag which they had occupied. When they left, Foppe came out of his hiding place: having heard the commotion downstairs, he had climbed out a window in the roof and hid in the narrow gutter.

Foppe Kuperus, 6 years old, before his appendectomy, which was considered to be a life-threatening surgery.

The next day the Germans returned. When Foppe's sister Tiete looked behind the house she saw him running "like a deer" in the field, already far from the Germans. She and their mother, Albertje, were met with the alarming sight of German soldiers crouching, aiming their guns and shooting at Foppe. Realizing that he was too far away, they gave up. Before they left they gave orders that, upon his return, he needed to appear before them at the Beetsterzwaag villa immediately.

Foppe had heard the bullets whiz past and continued to run quite a distance. He jumped into the only hiding place he saw: a ditch on the field's edge, filled with cold water from the spring rains. Covered with scratches from running through a barbed wire fence, he stayed in the ditch until he felt it was safe. Then he ran to a relative's home where he was given a change of clothes and a bike so he could return home quickly.

Albertje and Tiete passed along the Germans' orders, and Foppe reported to the Germans at the villa. There he joined Minne and John in a basement room where they were questioned. The Germans determined that they were telling the truth and brought them home. By this time, Minne and John had been away for four days. Foppe had developed a severe cold and the family feared pneumonia, but after several days of rest he recovered.

After the war the Kuperus family found out that their neighbors, the Van Zet family, had been deeply involved in the Dutch Resistance. Not only had they hid weapons, they also harbored Allied soldiers. It was the Van Zet home that the Germans were looking for on the evening they searched the Kuperus home.

Foppe's ration card, 1941

Reflections

The Meyers family: Henriet and Jim, Dan and Jessica, Kristen and Rob, Tim and Kendal

Henriet: Mom has been a wonderful example to us about living out our faith. She daily has devotions with meals and prays for her family, the community and the world. I remember observing Mom pray silently with her head bowed, her hands folded tightly and her lips moving softly in earnest prayer to our Heavenly Father.

Mom was a catechism teacher at Coopersville CRC. She rewarded students with Smarties when they memorized their lessons. Mom and Dad were mentors at Friendship Ministries for over ten years. She faithfully took part in Bible studies. Mom weekly visited shut-ins from her church at nursing homes or in their homes. We love you, Mom! Thank you for being a godly mother and grandmother who shows love to her family and to everyone she meets.

A round of Mens erger je niet! The English translation is "Man, don't annoy yourself!"

Jim: Mrs. Kuperus takes frugality to a whole new level. For instance, she saved the remainder of dish washing water in buckets to flush her toilet. Sometimes that backfired, as I've had to fish silverware out of the plumbing a few times.

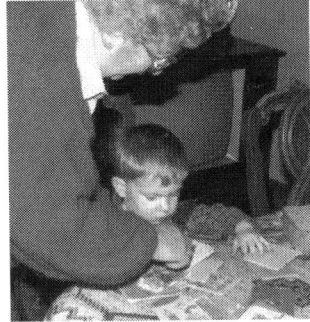

These books were greatly loved by the kids and grandkids.

Dan: I lived with Grandma one summer. She taught me this lesson on saving vs. spending money (in her words): "You know, Dan, you have to take every dollar and turn it over before you spend it or put it in your pocket." Great advice!

Kristen knitted the periodic table.

Kristen: I remember going to McDonald's Play Place with Grandma and having extra energy due to the sips of coffee she would serve us in the creamer cups – which was rationed from her Senior Coffee cup.

Tim: Grandma is extremely frugal, yet she remains very generous. She saves the dessert from her Sunset Manor meals and shares it with Kendal and me when we visit. When Grandma had a good deal at Meijer on her credit card, she shared the savings with Mom, Aunt Cindy and me. The receipt was over six feet long.

Josh, Jake and Rachel
Mike and Betty Epperly

Betty: Mom has always been upbeat, even while doing farm work. When we were young, she came in from from the barn in the morning to fix us a huge breakfast. Usually she wore dark green work pants (just like Dad's) and a sweatshirt (probably from the Ravenna flea market) on which was written a phrase she often repeated: "Kissing causes germs. Quick, make me sick!"

Mom's presence was invaluable when we brought our newborns home from the hospital. She had the "magic touch" with infants. When I was on bedrest with Jake's pregnancy, Mom came to our house in Livonia many weeks in a row to clean, cook, and take care of Josh. Every morning she brought my "medicine" upstairs – a roll of Double Salt Zoete drops and peanut butter on toast – with a cheerful smile. She took Josh on endless stroller rides, helping him add to his collections of acorns and pinecones. Doctors said there was a 99.5% chance that Jake would not survive the pregnancy. I know that Mom prayed earnestly every day for him and me, and he was born healthy and well. We could not have gotten through it without Mom's generous help.

Mike: I always looked forward to Mrs. K's visits. Not only was she great company, but we could count on her help with our projects.

When she visited us in Wisconsin we were in the middle of mulching. After it was dark we went to bed, but we kept hearing what sounded like metal scraping on concrete. Sure enough, when we looked outside, there she was in the dark, determined to finish the job until it was done.

Josh: One of my favorite photos of Grandma and me is the one of us dancing, with me standing on the table for the height difference. For as long as I can remember, Grandma has had an exhuberant free spirit that comes out especially with us grandkids. Even though she didn't let her own kids dance, she's willing to break a few rules for her grandkids.

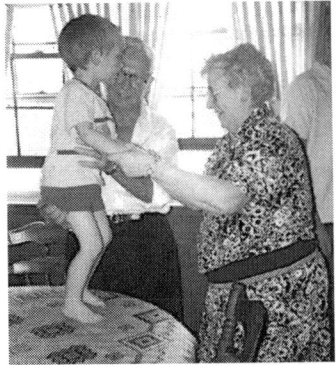

Jake: One Thanksgiving we each wrote something that we were thankful for on a card. We put the cards in a hat and everyone drew one. We sat in a circle and had a family prayer. Each person gave thanks for whatever was written on the card they picked. I, being the 4 year old I was, had written "Green Bay Packers football figurines." It was a very interesting wrap-up when Grandma ended the prayer with, "We are thankful for our Green Bay Packer figurines. Amen!"

Rachel: Grandma Kuperus is always available and willing to give. When my dad was undergoing tinnitus she spent a long period of time helping to care for me and my siblings at our house. After a long day spent cleaning, she would spend her night playing cards with me. I remember being excited whenever I'd come home from school and see her car parked in the driveway.

Cindy: Hard-working. Faithful. Determined. Unconventional. Although Mom was spared some of life's hardest trials, when faced with life's difficult circumstances, Mom did what needed to be done.

Cindy Kuperus

At a time when women her age were married and did not travel alone, Mom left her country and moved as a single woman to English-speaking North America. She made the most of what she was given.

A mother of five within nine years of marriage and also an active farmer's wife, Mom was up at 4:30 a.m. and in bed by 9:30 p.m. for years. She cooked, washed, house-kept, helped out in the barn, and was the primary caretaker of the children without any assistance from grandparents, mother's helpers, or the like. "Sick days" were unknown. It isn't surprising that I don't remember spending much time with Mom!

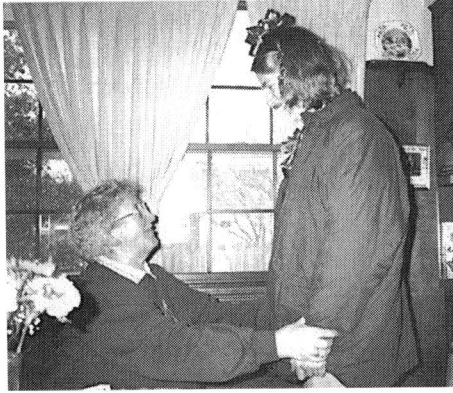

*Cindy flew in from New Jersey to
surprise me on my birthday.*

Something I have loved is Mom's contentedness with simplicity. She lives simply and frugally, and she finds joy in that. Her sense of humor and laughter often come out of simple things, too. There have been times that she has had private jokes that I have come upon. Once there was a small stuffed scarecrow in a corner of the garage. Mom found an old mug, and found a way for the scarecrow to hold the mug. It is possible that no one would ever see it, but mom would know it was there, and would smile I'm sure, when she would see it.

Mom is faithful to reading Scripture and prayer. When she prays aloud, I feel close to God because she prays with sincerity. That she prays for me daily is something that I am grateful for.

*When Cindy lived in Holland she was a
klompen dancer at the Tulip Festival.*

Tracy, Matt, Mark and Catherine Heun

Tracy: I feel so blessed to have my mom in my life. I know her to be faithful, dependable and kind-hearted. Mom has never fit the mold. Compared with other moms she was older, she was an immigrant, she worked in the barn alongside my dad, and she was funny (there aren't many 40 year olds who can pull off wearing a Fred Flintstone mask around the house and look amusing, not just weird). What influenced me positively was having this positive, smart, hard-working mom who expressed her faith genuinely, as my mother.

Mom is incredibly tough. Three months before she moved into Sunset, she decided to trim her hedges with an electric hedge clipper. She ended up severing the top of one of her fingers. I took her to the hospital, and we walked in with a much younger man who had nothing visibly wrong with him. This man and my mom were brought back into the ER at the same time.

When a nurse asked the man about his pain he answered, "I'm in so much pain, I can hardly stand it! You gotta help me out."

Mom's nurse asked her the same question, to which she replied, "Nothing. I feel no pain!"

The man's nurse asked him to rate his pain on a scale of 1 to 10, 10 being the worst. He said, "I'm at a 10. It's more than a 10!"

When Mom's nurse asked her the same question, Mom replied, "Zero. I feel no pain! When Mom was moved to the room where they sutured her finger, she began by asking the doctor to simply cut the tip of her finger off. "Wouldn't that be easiest?" she asked. The look on the doctor's face was priceless.

Matt: I have the utmost respect for people who uproot and move to a different country. When I think of Mrs. Kuperus, I think about the sacrifices that she made to come to the U.S., leaving behind friends and family in the Netherlands. I'm sure that few things were easy, but through faith, hard work, and sacrifice, she made a better life for her husband, her children, and herself. Thank you for your example!

Mark: When I think of Grandma Kuperus, I think of an upbeat, fun-loving little old Dutch lady. She's always looking on the positive side of things, and she's always looking to save a buck. Grandma never says no to a game. The first time she played Jenga with us she had to slow dance with a broom.

Catherine: One time we took Grandma someplace in our car. Mom and Dad were in the front, and Mark, Grandma and I were in the back seat. We were listening to a Prince CD. Grandma had no reaction to the slow songs, but when a rock song came on she was jamming, tapping her shoes against the floor and shaking her head to the beat.

Clay, Mike, LeRae and Miles Kuperus

Mike: Mom has been a steady, calm influence on our lives. She has demonstrated that hard work and living frugally can lead to financial success and that quietly caring about others and doing the right thing can lead to emotional peace and satisfaction. And while the last thing Mom would want is a spotlight on what a great Christ-centered life she has led, I can safely assume that when people are done reading about her, their overall impression will be that she is basically a saint.

But everyone has a breaking point, and teenagers will usually push someone to that point if anyone can. My long-term memory is lacking, but one vivid memory is when I pushed her too far. I believe it was when Dad had broken his leg from getting kicked by a cow, and all of us had to pick up some of the slack. This required me to get up very early before school to get things started with Mom. Of course I felt this was totally unfair, no one else would ever ask their kids to do such a thing, they should just hire someone with our excess fabulous wealth or whatever other teenage logic popped into my head. One morning I was whining and complaining as usual, and that was it. My stupidity and the pressure of trying to keep a farm running with Dad out of commission combined to finally crack Mom, and she came at me with a flurry of jabs, basically telling me to suck it up and do the work. Mom is not physically imposing and she wasn't trying to hurt me, so the physical impact was zero. Being a teenager, I was outraged that my Mom would do this to me, but by the time I got to the barn I saw how wrong I was to make a bad situation worse. Mom made me realize that it was just the way things were, due to circumstances, and I owed it to the family to deal with it.

Throughout life Mom has taken the bad in stride. She doesn't look to assign blame or dwell on how things could be different or how they are different for anyone else. Instead she immediately accepts things as they are and moves on to the next course of action. While this is one of many great attributes, it is probably one that has impacted me most. Some lessons you can teach people with words and actions, and others you just need to pound into them!

LeRae: I found it endearing when Jennie referred to me as "her favorite daughter-in-law," and though I was the only one, I felt deeply loved by her. Her help when our children were small was invaluable, especially when Clay was a toddler. Often I came home from work to a different house – one spic-and-span clean and tidy. I could count on 20 extra pairs of socks to be put away; she looked under beds and in closets to find the loners that had long been forgotten. Though her support has been greatly appreciated, it is her strength of character that has blessed me most. Her unrelenting faith – firmly trusting in God in times of plenty and in want – is one I hope to emulate in my own Christian walk.

Miles: What amazes me most about Grandma Jennie is her unfailing faith. Grandma continuously shines the light of Christ to whoever she comes into contact with. She has always been a role model Christian to me.

Clay: Grandma is sweet and kind of funny, and the best times I had with her was when I went to her house. Sometimes we play games, and when she loses she cries – I don't know if it's fake or not. She also brings me to McDonald's nearly every time I visit her, and sometimes I even watch Jeopardy with her. Then I sleep in that comfy side bed right next to her bed. I love to be with her.

References

Bolinger, Bruce. *Helpers of Allied Airmen – Dutch.* WWII Netherlands Escape Lines. Web. 28 Oct. 2015.

Châtel, Vincent and Chuck Ferree. *The Forgotten Camps: Ommen (Holland).* JewishGen – The Home of Jewish Geneology. Web. 4 Nov. 2015.

De Wind, Dorian. *What's In a Name? A Dutch Name, That Is.* 18 May 2009. Web. 18 Oct. 2015.

Erba, Eric M. and Andrew M. Novakovic. February, 1995. "The Evolution of Milk Pricing and Government Intervention in Dairy Production." E.B. 95-05. Department of Agricultural Economics, Cornell University. Ithaca, New York.

Trueman, C.N. *The Black Market.* Historylearningsite.co.uk. 20 Apr. 2015. Web. 10 Nov. 2015.

Warmbrunn, Werner. *The Dutch Under German Occupation, 1940-1945.* Stanford, California: Stanford University Press, 1963.

Woolf, Linda. "Survival and Resistance: The Netherlands Under Nazi Occupation." The United States Holocaust Museum, Washington, D.C., 6 Apr. 1999. Lecture.

51478458R00070

Made in the USA
Charleston, SC
20 January 2016